creative beading

creative beading

over 60 original jewellery projects and variations

Juju Vail

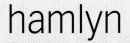

To my jewels: Orillia, Quinte and David
And my gems: Deb, Jen and Katie

First published in Great Britain in 2005 by
Hamlyn, a division of Octopus Publishing Group Ltd
2–4 Heron Quays, London E14 4JP

ISBN 0 600 61174 4
EAN 9780600611745

A CIP catalogue record for this book is available from the British Library

Printed and bound in China

10 9 8 7 6 5 4 3 2 1

contents

introduction

Beading is an absorbing hobby. You need very little equipment and the materials are a joy to collect and will provide much of the inspiration for your pieces. Beads are portable and do not require much storage or work space.

It is a pleasure to quickly make up a piece of jewellery to complement an outfit, or create a pair of earrings as a gift. Embarking on a larger project is also exciting because the beauty and colours of the beads reveal themselves as you work.

A love of beads is common to many of the world's cultures. However, each culture has its own tradition of bead making or trading, weaving and stringing. For many peoples, beads have a symbolic role as well as a decorative one. Lucky bead talismans are found throughout the world.

In Mediterranean cultures, beads with 'eye' patterns are said to protect against the 'evil eye', while 'worry' or prayer beads assist with religious ceremony. In Africa and the Americas, beads were used as currency with European traders and became symbols of wealth and power.

Beaded jewellery can be adapted to suit most people. When making jewellery as a gift or for yourself, select beads that are in scale with body size. Very large beads can overwhelm a petite person, while dainty jewellery can look lost on a larger figure. Most of the designs in this book can be adapted with this in mind.

The first section in the book introduces the tools, materials and fundamental techniques used throughout the projects. It also provides a pictorial reference of most sizes and styles of seed beads and an outline of other common bead types.

The projects in Beautiful Beginnings demonstrate several basic stringing and knotting techniques that are suitable for beginners. In Simple Charmers the range of basic techniques is expanded to include a beautiful charm bracelet and some quick and easy earrings and woven rings. More complex bead weaving is explained in Weaving Your Own Magic. The projects in this section show you how to make beaded beads, buttons and stars that can be used in other jewellery. The projects in the final section, Show Stoppers, may take more than one sitting to complete but make a significant statement. They include two intricate tassel necklaces, a beaded woven bracelet and beaded bead earrings.

Beading is a versatile, practical and creative craft – enjoy!

tools and materials

Many people adopt beading as a hobby because it requires so few tools. String or thread, scissors and beads are the only essentials. However, it does not take long for most beaders to find that they can never have enough beads! Making coordinating bead puddles of different colours, shapes and sizes is a delicious way to spend an afternoon.

The tools used in the projects have been limited to those you will need most frequently. You will not need them all for every project so collect them as you work your way through the book.

The extensive picture dictionary of beads (see pages 14–19) will help you to know what to look for when you go bead shopping. You will find it particularly useful if you shop over the Internet, where you cannot always see the difference between types of beads.

tools

The following is a list of the basic tools you will need for beading.

Small sharp scissors (1) You will need a good pair of scissors to trim threads close to your beading work. Nail scissors are very good for this purpose.

Flush wire cutters (2) Essential for trimming eyepins, headpins and beading wire.

Needle-nose pliers (3) Useful for gently coaxing needles through beads filled with thread as well as for bending wires. Try to buy the best pair you can afford.

Round-nose pliers (4) Used for bending wire into an eye shape. Choose a pair with variation in diameter from the tip to the base so that you can select how large your eye shapes are.

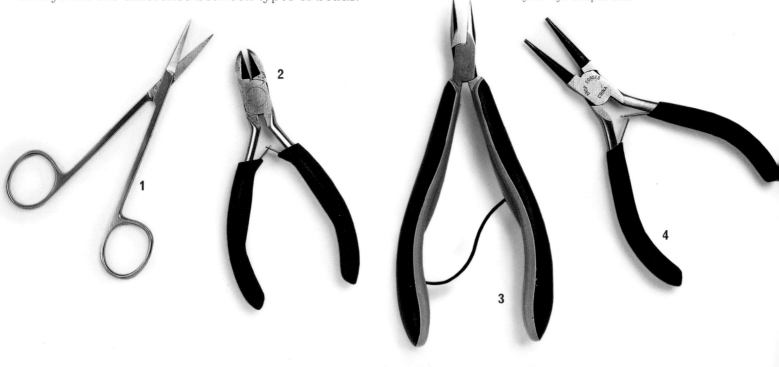

Crimping pliers (5) Specialist pliers that curl and flatten crimp beads. Wide-nosed pliers will flatten crimp beads adequately, but crimping pliers curve the bead, making it smoother for the wearer.

Clear plastic ruler and measuring tape (6) To measure thread and strands of beads while you are working.

White flannel cloth Working on a cloth rather than directly on the tabletop prevents the beads from rolling around. Lay piles of seed beads on the cloth and use a teaspoon to scoop leftover beads back into their containers.

T-pin A T-pin is just like a straight pin but with a bar on top instead of a round or oval head. It is useful for knotting thread close to a bead hole.

Small clamps or clips (7) When you are not working on a strand it is essential to clamp it in order to secure the beads. You can use stationery clips or clothes pegs and also small clips found in electronic shops, but be sure to choose ones with no teeth so that you will not damage the beading cords.

Bead reamer (8) This enlarges stone and pearl holes when you need to fit two threads through. You can buy electric bead reamers but a simple hand one is perfect for occasional use.

Stopper bead Not strictly a piece of equipment but useful nonetheless. A stopper bead is an ordinary bead that stops the beads falling off the thread when there is no knot. It also helps to

maintain tension while you are working. Use a bead in a different colour so that you remember to remove it when your work is complete. Bring your needle through the stopper bead and back round through the same side again. Begin your work.

Firm cushion Pinning your work to a cushion while you weave will help you to maintain tension.

Good lighting It is essential to be able to clearly see your tiny beads and the eye in your needle. Make sure you work in a bright area with no shadows.

needles

Beading needles (1) Available in several sizes, beading needles are longer and more flexible than dressmaker's needles. They are useful for beading fringes and when stringing necklaces with nylon thread.

1

Sharps needles (2) These are shorter and more rigid than beading needles. They are great for beading beads and buttons. The higher the needle size number, the finer the needle. Fine needles break easily, so always have extras to hand. Needle size 12 is suitable for beads size 10° to 14°. Needle size 13 is suitable for beads size 10° to 15°. Needle sizes 15 and 16 are suitable for beads smaller than 14°.

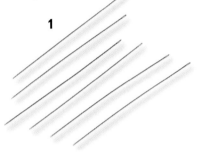

2

Twisted wire needles (3) These have a large eye so they are easier to thread than sharps and beading needles, however, they are not as rigid, which can make weaving more difficult.

3

threads and cords

Nylon beading thread (1) Used when beading with lightweight beads such as seed beads. It can be used to string a light necklace as well as weave beads. Nylon beading thread is strong and drapes well. It comes in many colours and various sizes. The smallest size is 00, for beads size 16° and smaller. Size 0 is for beads 14° and smaller, size B is for beads between 11° and 15°, and size D is for beads between 6° and 12°. Be aware that some older glass beads and some metal beads, although not heavy, have sharp edges that may cut the nylon threads over time. It may be more suitable to weave or string these with beading wire or fishing line.

1

Silk cord (2–4) Silk cords can be bought with a ready attached needle, in a variety of sizes and colours. Thread made from twisted strands of silk is traditionally used for stringing pearls and light gems and silk is said to have the best drape of any fibre.

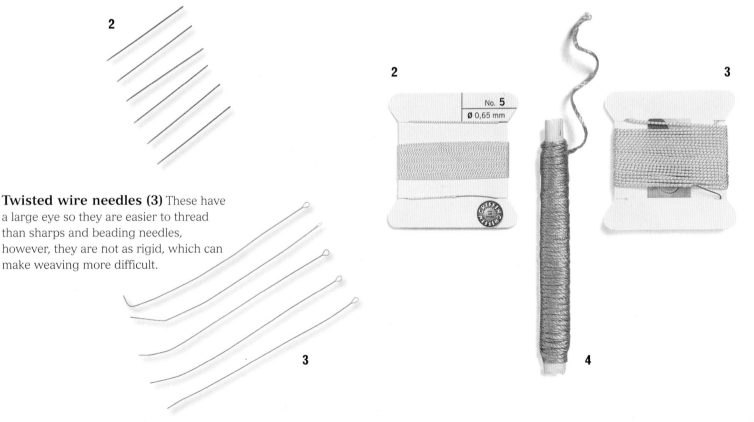

2

No. **5**
Ø 0,65 mm

3

4

Linen beading threads (5) Linen thread holds good knots and is useful for necklaces that include macramé knotting (see pages 43–44).

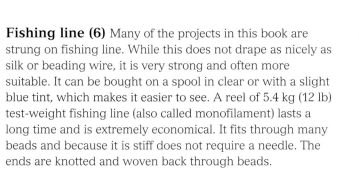

Beading wire (7) There are several brands of beading wire available. It is made of many tiny wire filaments wrapped in a smooth coating. It is strong, drapes nicely and comes in many colours and finishes. A crimp bead is crushed around it to finish the work because it does not knot. It is a good alternative to fishing line but can be costly.

Fishing line (6) Many of the projects in this book are strung on fishing line. While this does not drape as nicely as silk or beading wire, it is very strong and often more suitable. It can be bought on a spool in clear or with a slight blue tint, which makes it easier to see. A reel of 5.4 kg (12 lb) test-weight fishing line (also called monofilament) lasts a long time and is extremely economical. It fits through many beads and because it is stiff does not require a needle. The ends are knotted and woven back through beads.

Cords of nylon (8), rubber and leather (9) These come in many sizes and colours, and are often used to hang a single pendant. They can also be used in strung and knotted necklaces for a less traditional look than silk cord.

wax

Beeswax (1) Wax is used to condition nylon threads. It makes the thread stronger, easier to maintain a firm tension, and less likely to become tangled. It is best used when working with a doubled thread as it helps the two ends to stick together. After threading your needle, run the thread through the wax and then through your fingers to remove excess wax.

Thread conditioner (2) Synthetic thread conditioner is available as an alternative to beeswax. It prevents the thread ends from sticking to one another and becoming tangled. Use it in the same manner as wax when working with a single thread.

1

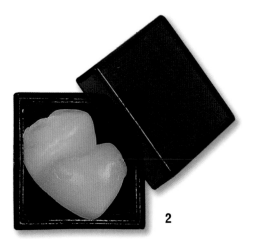

2

adhesives

Instant-bond glue (1) Used throughout the projects in this book to hold the knots of strung necklaces.

Liquid seam sealant (3) When bead weaving, the tip of the needle is dipped in seam sealant before ending a thread. As the needle goes through the final beads, the sealant rubs off and helps to keep the thread ends in place.

1

2

Epoxy glue (2) For holding non-porous materials together, such as pin backs to buttons. Use in a well-ventilated area.

3

findings

'Findings' is the name given to the many different metal pieces used for attaching jewellery parts together and to the body. Some of them make great features in themselves.

Closures (1) Used for fastening necklaces and bracelets, closures are available in many styles and sizes.

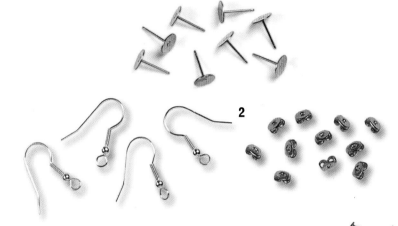

Earring wires and **earring posts (2)** These come in silver, gold, plated, brass and surgical-steel styles. It is advisable to avoid the brass and plated ones because they can cause ear infections. Use the best you can afford.

Headpins and **Eyepins (3)** Used to make bead dangles. They too come in a variety of metals. Choose one to suit your bead colour.

Jump rings (4) These rings attach one part of a piece of jewellery to another.

Crimp beads (5) Soft metal beads that are crushed around beading wire in place of knots to secure beads in place. They come in a variety of metal finishes.

Clam-shell bead tips (6) Shaped like a clam, these bead tips conceal knots and crimp beads at the ends of strands.

know your beads

There are many different types and styles of beads. Anything with a hole in it can be used. Seeds, bones, wood, nuts, glass, stones and plastics are all used as bead materials.

The number of different semi-precious stone beads and the cuts they come in is astounding. A guideline to some of the main shapes is illustrated here.

Tiny seed beads, also known as rocailles, are an important subsection of beads. The illustrations on pages 16–17 will give you an idea of many of the styles. Be aware that not all colours are permanent. Ask the seller for information.

pearls

Pearls are available in many colours, shapes and qualities. Today, most pearls are cultured, which means humans introduce an irritant into the oyster's shell to make it produce nacre in the shape of a pearl. Differently shaped beads are introduced as irritants, and these result in the different pearl shapes that are available. Pearls come in a wide variety of natural and colour-treated shades, including neutrals such as silver, cream and brown, and outlandish colours like pistachio, peacock and lavender. Some of the most popular shapes and styles are shown here.

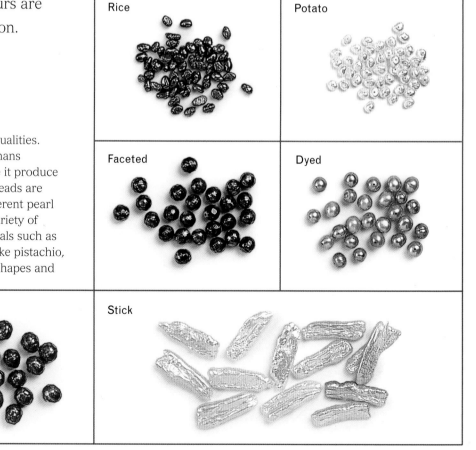

Rice

Potato

Faceted

Dyed

Faceted potato

Stick

glass and stones

The following shapes and cuts are commonly available in glass and stones. When buying beads, bear in mind that hole sizes vary a lot and consider what thread or wire you will use. If the hole is big, you may need to put smaller beads or bead caps on either side of the bead to prevent it from moving about. If you plan to use cord you will need to choose beads with larger holes.

Cabochon	Bi/Pi or doughnut bead	Faceted	Smooth
Pressed glass	Carved stone	Crow and pony beads	Briolette and pear shaped
Faceted nugget	Chip	Cubes and rectangles	Top drilled drop
Nugget	Rose montee	Coin	Rondelle

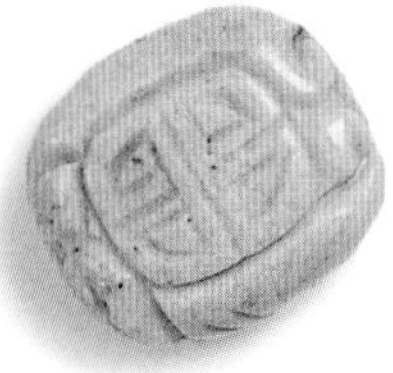

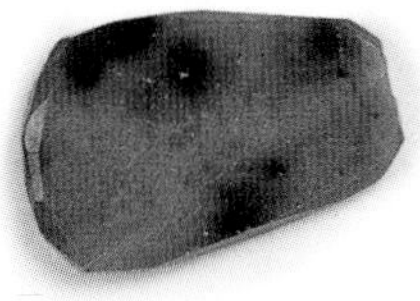

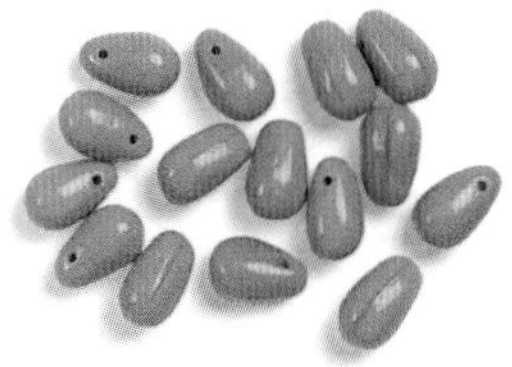

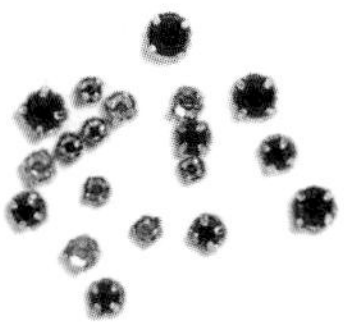

seed beads

Seed beads are usually made of glass. They are used for bead weaving, to string jewellery and to provide spacers for larger beads. They come in a variety of sizes and shapes. The size number is indicated by an ° symbol sometimes written as /0, pronounced 'ought'. The larger the number, the smaller the size of bead. Therefore, an 8° (8/0) is much larger than a 14° (14/0) bead. The following is a list of approximate sizes and weights for the most commonly used beads.

6°	10 beads per 2.5 cm (1 in)	17 beads per gram (⅟₁₆ oz)
8°	8 beads per 2.5 cm (1 in)	48 beads per gram (⅟₁₆ oz)
11°	17 beads per 2.5 cm (1 in)	100 beads per gram (⅟₁₆ oz)
14°	26 beads per 2.5 cm (1 in)	256 beads per gram (⅟₁₆ oz)

However, different makers list their beads as slightly different sizes. The examples of beaded peyote strips on page 23 are made up entirely of size 11° beads but there is a great deal of variation in the size as is evident in the uneven shape of the weaving. Furthermore, two beads of the same size may have radically different-sized holes, which will affect the ease of use when bead weaving. Your supplier should be able to advise you.

Seed beads are often bought in increments of 5 g (³⁄₁₆ oz). In many of the projects, 5 g (³⁄₁₆ oz) has been specified as a quantity. This will be more than enough to finish the project.

bead shapes

There are two main shapes of tiny beads. Doughnut-shaped, which are often referred to as sead beads, are quite rounded, and then there are the Japanese-made cylinder-shaped beads. Each bead looks different when woven and each shape has a particular use. 'Charlottes', 'tri-cuts', 'hex cuts' and 'true cuts' all refer to doughnut-shaped beads that have had one or more sides cut off. This provides a subtle sparkle like a gem cut. Some of the most popular shapes of beads are shown here.

Hex cut (11°)

Nail head

Hex cut (14°)

True cut (15°)

Steel cut

Charlotte (13°)

Bugle

Japanese delica (11°)

Iridescent tri cut (15°)

Opaque (8°)

bead finishes

In addition to the shape, there are a variety of finishes that will influence the final appearance of beads. They may be transparent, semi-transparent or opaque. Each of these conditions can be coloured or clear. In some cases, a transparent clear glass bead will have a coloured lining that will be visible through the glass. The core of the bead can also be lined with a silver or copper foil, which reflects light.

The firing of the glass can cause changes in the appearance of beads. They can take on iridescent effects in many different colours. Beads may also be treated after firing to change the surface appearance to a matt glass. Some of the most popular finishes are shown here.

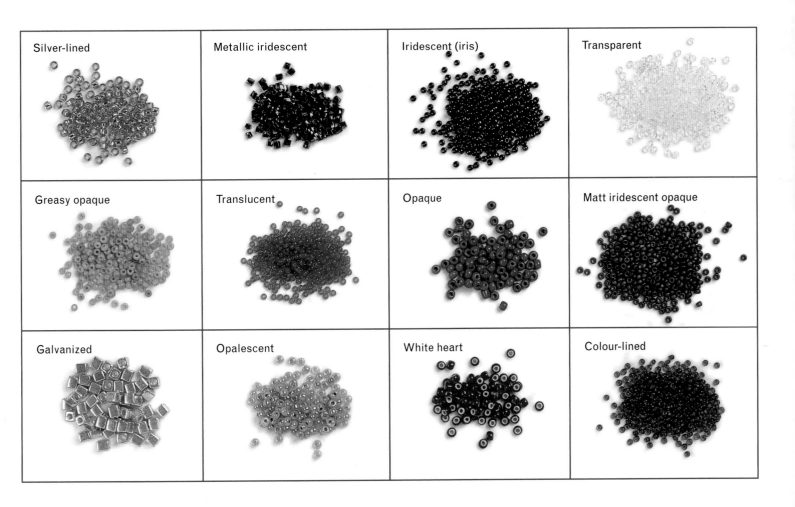

Silver-lined

Metallic iridescent

Iridescent (iris)

Transparent

Greasy opaque

Translucent

Opaque

Matt iridescent opaque

Galvanized

Opalescent

White heart

Colour-lined

metal

Metal beads can make your work look as though a metalsmith has crafted it. Beautiful silver beads are handmade in Thailand and Bali, Indonesia. Handmade 19k and 24k gold beads are also available. Brass, copper and silver beads are available new and antique, particularly from Africa. Be aware that these metals may discolour and also cause irritation to some people.

Cheaper 'metal' beads are available in the form of cast pewter beads and plated plastic beads. The coating may chip off and the silver and gold colours are not very realistic, but the beads are lightweight, which may be an advantage in some designs.

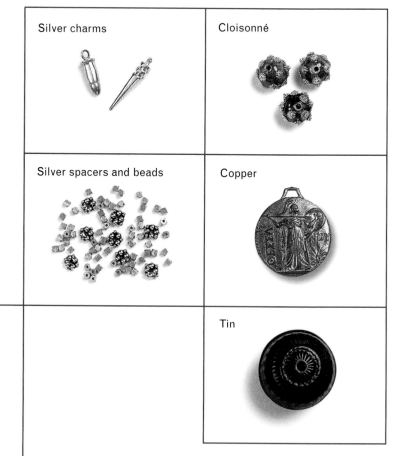

Silver charms

Cloisonné

Silver spacers and beads

Copper

Tin

Artists' glass beads

African trade beads

Vintage Czechoslovakian glass

Italian murrini

glass

Glass beads date back thousands of years and come in a huge variety of forms. Contemporary glass beads are either handmade with a torch flame, or pressed into shape using a kiln. They come in so many different finishes that they often look like another material, such as a gemstone.

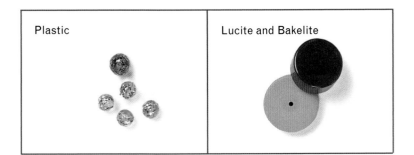

Plastic

Lucite and Bakelite

plastic

Plastic beads come in many qualities. The varieties that are available in craft stores for children's jewellery represent one end of the scale, while vintage Bakelite and Lucite are collected and sought after. Sometimes the colour and qualities of plastic are unique. Do not disregard plastic, no matter how precious your jewellery piece.

other materials

Wood, bone, shells, lacquer and leather are examples of less common bead materials. Bone and horn beads must be one of the oldest forms of adornment known to man.

buttons as beads

Buttons can make wonderful beads. Some older forms such as cut steel and glass look like no other bead available. You need to work around a button's one-sidedness and shank when designing with it. However, this characteristic can be an advantage in some pieces of jewellery, such as bracelets and choker necklaces.

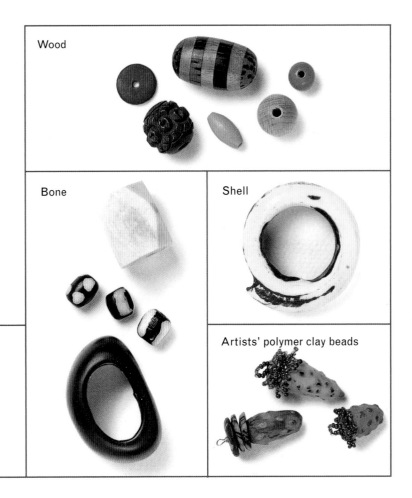

Wood

Bone

Shell

Artists' polymer clay beads

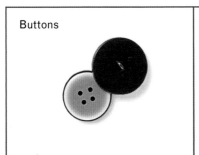

Buttons

Carved nut

techniques

Every project in this book includes illustrations of specific techniques used, but there are a few techniques you will repeat many times, such as square knots and weaving in ends. This section also includes instructions for several basic weaving methods, and shows how to work them in a flat square. The weaves can also be worked in tubes, circles and other shapes and these will be demonstrated in the relevant projects.

beginning a new thread

When beginning a new thread always leave a 10 cm (4 in) tail to work into the beading later. If you are beginning a new thread part way through the work, weave in and out of a few beads before you begin adding new beads so that you have a secure end against which to work. This will give even tension over the whole of your work. Leave a 10 cm (4 in) tail as usual to knot and weave into your work later.

thread end   beginning tail

weaving in ends

Whenever you have finished a piece of bead weaving or a necklace strand, you cannot trim the thread ends too close to the knot, in case the knot works its way undone. To avoid this problem, weave the thread ends back through the last few beads. The illustration above shows the thread end and beginning tail, woven back into the beadwork before they are trimmed off. In the illustration below, the ends of a necklace have been woven back through beads after they have been knotted or secured with crimp beads.

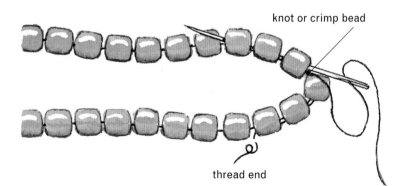

knot or crimp bead

thread end

square knot

This knot is used in necklace strands and bead weaving to secure the threading material. Beginning with two thread ends, overlap them, with thread A on top. Fold the A end underneath thread B and bring it back over the top of B. Lay thread A (which is now coming from the right-hand side) over thread B, in through the knot and then bring it out towards you and pull the ends tight. This sequence will give you a secure knot.

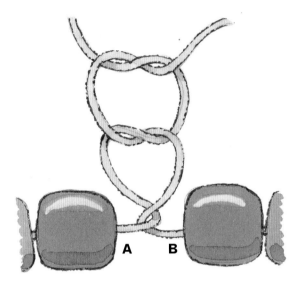

overhand knot

This knot is used between beads in traditional pearl necklaces to keep the beads apart and protect the delicate pearls from rubbing against each other. It is used in other types of necklace too, because it provides a nice articulation and helps the necklace to drape well. It can be made with one or more strands. Make a loop and pass the working end through it. Pull the ends to tighten the knot.

half-hitch and double half-hitch knots

These knots are used in jewellery with macramé cording and they can be worked with different colours and more threads. Typically, four threads are secured to a cushion with a pin or attached to a board with nails in it. The two centre threads are held taut while the outside threads alternate forming loops over and under them. These are pulled tight forming a boxy knot. In the half-hitch knot (below, left) the thread on the left will always go over (or under) the threads in the middle, creating a spiral, whereas the double half-hitch knot (below, right) will have the left-hand thread alternating over and under the middle threads each time it is worked.

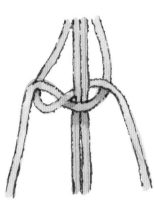

buttonhole stitch

Used in beading to cover cords, buttonhole stitch provides an attractive stitched finish and strengthens the cord. It is often done in a contrasting colour or type of thread. The buttonhole thread is brought down over the cord, and then up behind it, crossing in front of the buttonhole thread to create a loop.

brick stitch

Brick stitch, sometimes known as 'Comanche weave' is used in this book in the tassel for the Tickled Pink Tassel on pages 118–121, but there are many other ways to use it as well. It makes a firm fabric with staggered, brick-like beads.

Begin with a foundation row as shown in the illustration. The amount of beads you use will depend on how wide you want your weave to be. String one bead and then pass through the closest exposed loop of the foundation row. Pass back up through the same bead and continue, adding one bead at a time in this manner.

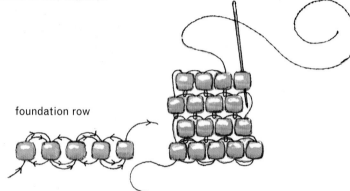

foundation row

right-angle weave

Right-angle weave is the only construction method that sets the beads at right angles. It produces a slightly open, flexible fabric. To make right-angle weave, begin with a foundation of four beads joined in a circle. Add three beads in a figure of eight movement. For subsequent rows, first add three beads and then two beads.

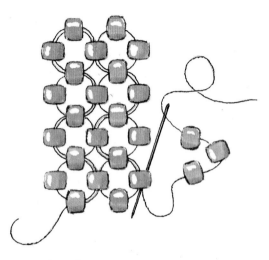

peyote stitch

Peyote stitch is the most commonly used weaving stitch. It produces a more flexible fabric than brick stitch. It is also sometimes known as 'one-bead netting', 'one-drop' and 'two-drop' (which are slight variations) or 'gourd stitch' (when it is worked in the round). It can also be worked in a flat circle, known as circular peyote, as in the beaded buttons on pages 88–91.

Make a foundation row by stringing an even number of beads, twice the number you want in one row. Pick up a new bead and bring your needle back through the second to last bead. Pick up another bead, skip a bead in your foundation row and go through the next bead. Continue like this to the end of the row. The beads will fall into a castellated line.

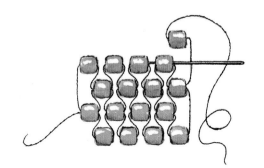

square stitch

Square stitch produces a firm, strong fabric. The beads stack up directly above each other, making it an easy stitch to use when following a pattern on graph paper. It can be worked by adding one bead at a time or two beads at a time as in the Jewel Jangles project (see pages 122–125). The one-bead version is illustrated here.

Begin by stringing a foundation row of beads. For the second row, string two beads, then pass the thread through the second to last bead of the first row, and back through the second bead of those just strung. Continue by stringing one bead, passing through the third to last bead of the first row, and back through the bead just strung. Repeat this looping technique across to the end of the row.

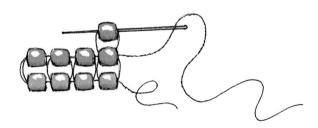

colour combining beads

When choosing colours for projects with lots of seed beads, work with a controlled colour palette, extending your bead choice with a variety of finishes. It is very easy when looking at all the gorgeous little packages of beads to want to use them all. Bear in mind that when you wear a piece of jewellery, it will usually be seen at a greater distance than your beading table. All those tiny seed beads can merge like a pointillist painting. Try using colours near each other on the colour wheel (right), known as harmonious colours. For example, if you want to use predominantly blue, accent it with either greens and turquoise or purples and some reds. Stay away from mixing a complementary colour, those colours that are opposite each other on the colour wheel, such as blue with orange, unless you are trying to achieve a brownish, neutral look.

When choosing seed bead finishes, try combining matt with sparkly beads. If you put silver-lined beads next to iridescent or cut seed beads the look can be overwhelming, whereas a well-chosen silver-lined accent bead will glint enticingly when mixed into a ground of mostly matt opaque beads.

To judge the effect of seed beads together you need to see them without the holes showing. Thread a few onto some fishing line to see how they look. If you are planning work on a larger project, you may like to weave yourself a small peyote stitch sampler of 10 beads wide and about 10 cm (4 in) long. Alternatively, make yourself a quick beaded bead or button in your chosen colour scheme; you can then use it in your final piece.

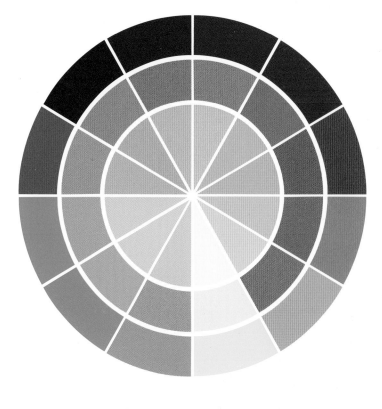

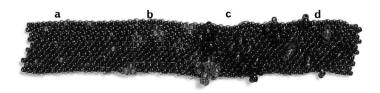

Three colours are used to decorate the peyote weave; frosted, silver-lined orange, transparent red, and transparent pink. They are used in:

- **a** Single bead dots
- **b** Four bead dots
- **c** Four beads embellished with 3 beads each
- **d** A single bead embellished with 3 beads

When used as single dots they are barely visible but provide a subtle change in colour. The silver-lined bead glints from the opaque orange background. They all show up well when used to embellish.

This peyote stitch strip is striped with a wide variety of close-coloured beads.

beautiful beginnings

These quick and easy projects will introduce you to the basic skills needed to make your own beaded creations. They demonstrate versatile techniques that you can employ with different types of beads in many styles of jewellery.

The techniques shown in this chapter will also give you the foundations to make and repair many pieces of classic jewellery. These include pearl knotting, which is used in the Many Moons project (see pages 26–29), and beading with wire and crimp beads, as in the Stepping Stones project (see pages 46–49). Macramé knotting and button closures are shown in the Spots and Stripes necklace on pages 42–45, while Going Dotty (see pages 38–41) demonstrates a quick way to make up a bracelet or choker necklace. The Turquoise Danglers on pages 34–37 show you how to whip up a pair of earrings in no time. Remember, many of these projects can be adapted to make longer pieces of jewellery or shortened to make a bracelet.

many moons

variations pendant string and
candy-coloured necklace

Pearls have a lustre and beauty
unmatched by other beads and it is
easy to see why they have always been so
popular. Today they come in a huge variety of
colours, shapes and sizes. Here, a mixture of real
and glass pearls in white, cream, champagne and bronze
shades have been strung together with a mother-of-pearl
button closure.

This project requires a beading needle that comes with the silk attached
(see page 10). These are usually sold in 2 m (6½ ft) lengths. You will want
the needle to remain attached to the silk when you finish, as you may
have enough left to complete a second necklace. If you detach the needle,
you will need to rethread the silk onto a beading needle and this will
make it impossible to thread through the tiny holes in most pearls.

before you begin

materials

60 x glass and real pearls, between 5 mm
(³⁄₁₆ in) and 10 mm (³⁄₈ in) in size, in a
variety of colours such as white, cream,
champagne, apricot, soft pink and bronze

50 x 11° seed beads in pearl white

1 x 17 mm (¹¹⁄₁₆ in) mother-of-pearl two-
hole button

2 m (6½ ft) length of beading silk with
needle, size no. 5

tools

Scissors
Long hatpin or T-pin
Fine twisted wire needle
Needle-nose pliers (optional)
Instant-bond glue

making the necklace

1 Make a knot 10 cm (4 in) from the tail end of the thread. String on one 5 mm (³⁄₁₆ in) pearl followed by enough seed beads to form a loop large enough to fit the button through (approximately 30). Push the beads to the centre of the thread then put the needle back through the 5 mm (³⁄₁₆ in) pearl. You now have two threads.

3 Continue beading by stringing a pearl and then making an overhand knot until the necklace is 45–50 cm (18–20 in) long. End with a small pearl that will fit a thread through twice and make a knot.

4 Make a button shank to attach the button to the necklace. String eight seed beads then thread up through the first buttonhole, down through the second, and string eight more seed beads. Make a square knot as close to the last pearl as you can and work your thread back down through the pearl. Trim the thread and squeeze a tiny drop of glue on the knot before the shank.

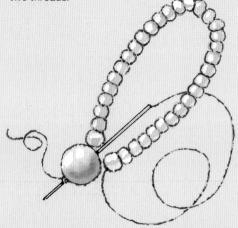

2 Make a square knot (see page 21) with the two threads, pushing the knot close to the pearl. String another pearl and make an overhand knot (see page 21) with the single thread. Insert a pin through your knot into the bead hole and tighten the knot, using the pin to ensure the knot lies right next to your bead. This technique can take some practice but it is worth getting right because you will use it repeatedly. You may find it easier to anchor your necklace as you knot, by pinning the buttonhole loop to a cushion.

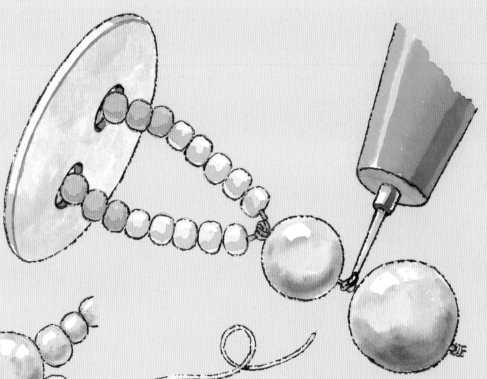

5 Using the twisted wire needle, work the first tail of the thread end through the next pearl, trim, and put a drop of glue on the last knot.

variations pendant string and candy-coloured necklace

pendant string

Any knotted necklace can hang a pendant if the pendant loop is large enough to slide over the biggest bead. In this necklace, assortments of opaque and transparent glass beads have been used and seed beads with large holes have covered the knots.

candy-coloured necklace

Brightly coloured vintage glass and plastic beads look stunning with this number button, which can be worn to the side so it is visible from the front. Look on the Internet for vintage beads.

fairy chain bracelet

variations star charm bracelet and double-strand necklace

This bracelet makes a wonderful gift. It can be made in under an hour and there are endless variations in style. You can achieve quite different looks depending on the beads you choose; an eclectic mix of beads such as those used in the project lends a contemporary appeal, or you could use beaded stars to turn this project into a charm bracelet (see page 33, top). The design can easily be lengthened to wear wrapped around your wrist twice or made even longer to become an eye-catching, double-strand necklace (see page 33, bottom).

before you begin

materials

1 x 12 mm (½ in) button

1 m (39 in) length of clear fishing line

5 g (³⁄₁₆ oz) 11° seed beads in pink, opalescent pink and mauve

8 x 4 mm (³⁄₁₆ in) beads in complementary colours: used here are ivory faceted pearls, opals, pink plastic glitter beads, vintage Japanese snowball glass beads, and pink and white fibre-optic beads

14 x 8–12 mm (⁵⁄₁₆–½ in) beads in complementary colours: used here are ivory ceramic beads, vintage pink flower beads, and lozenge-shaped pink plastic beads

4 x 15–20 mm (⁹⁄₁₆–¹³⁄₁₆ in) beads in complementary colours: used here are cut-crystal white Czech bicones, stick pearls, vintage Japanese glass, and polymer-clay beads

tools

Needle-nose pliers (optional)

Scissors

Small clothes peg or clamp

Instant-bond glue

making the bracelet

1 Attach a clamp to one end of the fishing line to stop the threaded beads from falling off. String approximately 25 seed beads into the centre of the line. They should form a loop big enough to form the button closure.

2 Remove the clamp, hold the two ends of line together and thread three small beads onto them to make a 'bead grouping' of about 1.5 cm (⅝ in). Check that the loop can fit over the button. Clamp one end of the fishing line.

3 Begin threading a mixture of seed and larger beads onto the unclamped line. Aim for a balance of size and colours across the length. Work until you have about 16.5 cm (6½ in) of beaded line including the loop (or 2.5 cm (1 in) less than your finished length). Clamp this line.

4 Begin threading the second strand, holding it next to the first to be sure you are balancing the sizes and shapes of the beads.

5 Pull both lines together and thread about three larger beads onto the two lines together. The length of the bracelet should now be 18 cm (7 in) – or within 1 cm (⅜ in) of the finished length.

6 Thread five seed beads with good-sized holes onto each strand. Bring one strand up through each buttonhole (from back of button to front). Bring each strand through three seed beads on top of the button and back down through the opposite holes. This is a good time to gently try on the bracelet for size.

7 Bring each strand back down through the five seed beads and make a square knot (see page 21). Thread both ends through the first bead in your larger-bead grouping and make another square knot. Repeat this for each bead in the grouping and then push the threads through the first 2 cm (⅜ in) of beads on each strand.

8 Cut the line at both ends. Add a drop of glue on a knot between one of the beads in the grouping.

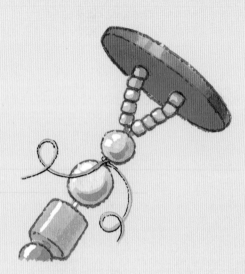

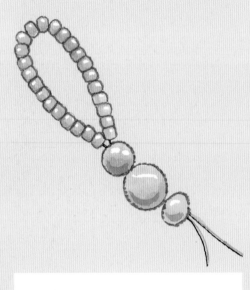

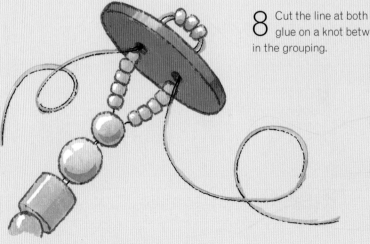

tip

✳ This bracelet is designed to fit close to the wrist so that it does not dangle in front of the palm and get in the way. These measurements will make a bracelet 19 cm (7½ in) long – a good size for most wrists. To adapt the size, first measure around your wrist, and then add 3–4 cm (1–1½ in).

variations star charm bracelet and double-strand necklace

star charm bracelet

Turn to page 95 to learn how to make beaded stars and, using head- and eyepins to make charms, turn this project into a charm bracelet.

double-strand necklace

To make a double-stranded necklace, increase the length to twice the circumference of your wrist plus 7–8 cm (2½–3 in). When trying it on for fit, check that the balance of colours and sizes works well over the two strands.

These earrings play with the different colours of natural turquoise, which can vary from green to blue. The blue turquoise star is combined with a green glass bead while the green turquoise star hangs from a blue glass bead. Natural turquoise works beautifully with glass and is often used to great effect with sterling silver. The earrings are finished with a clam-shell bead tip, which is also useful for attaching swinging multiple strands as in our variation, or for stones that have a hole running sideways through the top as in the Chalcedony Drop Earrings (see pages 56–59).

turquoise danglers
variations multi-strand danglers and spots and stripes earrings

before you begin

materials

2 x 2.5 cm (1 in) long, diamond-shaped glass
beads, of slightly different green colours
2 x 1.5 cm (⅝ in) turquoise stars of varying
shades
2 sterling silver earring wires
2 clam-shell bead tips
10 x 11° seed beads in brown and striped
pattern
1 small glass blue bead
1 small glass green bead
Nylon beading thread, size D

tools

Needle-nose pliers
Size 12 sharps needle
Scissors
Beeswax
Instant-bond glue

making the earrings

1 Thread the needle with a length of waxed nylon thread. Working with doubled thread, string one seed bead, which will be invisible inside the clam-shell bead tip. Make an overhand knot (see page 21) with the seed bead trapped in the middle.

3 Make a double knot with the other end and pull it next to the bead, inside the clam-shell bead tip. Allow your beads to hang with a little slackness below the clam-shell bead tip.

tip

* To open the loop on the earring wire, always move the end to one side with a pair of pliers rather than opening the circle.

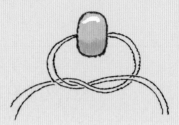

2 Take the needle and thread down through one clam-shell bead tip, one small glass bead, one long glass bead, three seed beads, one turquoise star and one more seed bead. Come back up through the star and other beads and out through the clam-shell bead tip.

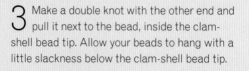

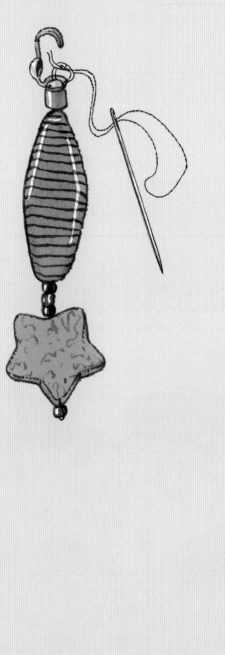

4 Drop glue on the knot then trim the thread ends. Close the clam-shell bead tip gently with the pliers. Open the loop on the earring wires and slip on the loop of the clam-shell bead tip. Close the earring wire loops.

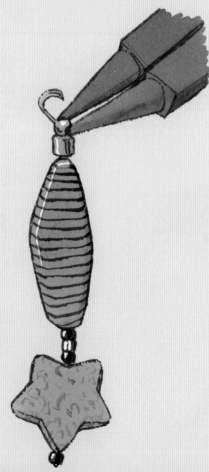

variations multi-strand danglers and spots and stripes earrings

multi-strand danglers

Several strands of seed beads can be hung from one bead tip to make an earring with lots of movement. To do this, thread each strand separately and make a knot with all the strands inside the bead tip. Use nylon thread for seed beads and lightweight beads, or lightweight bead wire for heavier stones or glass beads. Use a large crimp bead to fasten the strands together inside the bead tip.

spots and stripes earrings

These earrings follow the same beading pattern as the main project but use different beads. The green striped beads are pressed Czech glass while the spotted beads are new American glass. The same beading pattern can be used with smaller beads to make a more delicate earring.

going dotty
variation bracelet with dangles

This bracelet is strung on memory wire, which reshapes itself to a consistent circumference. It comes in several sizes to fit wrists, necks, fingers and even wineglass stems. Because it reshapes itself, no fastener is needed which makes it the easiest way to string beads. Wire ends are simply bent to prevent the beads from falling off, while the shape of the wire conforms without closures to your wrist, finger or neck. Memory wire can also be used for choker-style necklaces, but a simple closure may be needed due to the heavier distribution of beads at the front of the necklace.

before you begin

materials

6 loops of memory wire 6.5 cm (2½ in)
   in diameter
1 x 90 cm (35 in) strand of 'Christmas Beads'
   or other mixture of seed beads

tools

Heavy wire cutters
Round-nose pliers

making the bracelet

1 Curl one end of the memory wire as follows: place the tip in the mouth of the round-nose pliers with no wire poking out of the top.

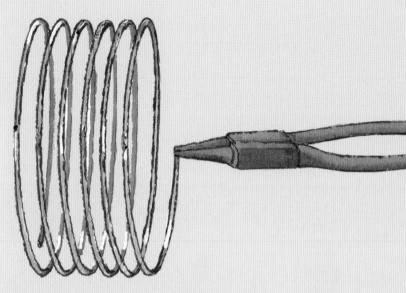

2 Rotate the pliers so that the wire curls into a loop in the same direction as the curve of its memory. Make the loop with two complete coils.

3 String beads on the wire from the other end until you have six complete coils, leaving about 2 cm (¾ in) of wire. With such a mixture of bead colour, random arrangements work perfectly well, but try to avoid putting too many similar beads together because the block of colour will stand out on the finished bracelet.

4 Twist the end of the wire twice around the pliers as before to complete the bracelet.

tips

✳ Memory wire needs to go around your wrist at least three times if you are using heavier beads, as in the bracelet with dangles on page 41.

✳ 'Christmas beads' is the name for this mixture of striped and plain bright seed beads. Look for them at dealers who sell African trade beads.

variation bracelet with dangles

This example uses larger beads but fewer coils. It also includes a couple of dangles. These can be made on headpins or eyepins (see Charming Bracelet for instructions, pages 64–67), and then threaded onto the beading wire between beads. Make sure they are evenly distributed.

spots and stripes
variation four-strand necklace

To make a necklace from beads with large holes, but without the formal look of knots between each bead, you can either string your beads on a leather cord or you can use a waxed linen or nylon string with macramé ends, as shown here. This design has the advantage of not distributing any beads at the back of the neck, where they may be uncomfortable, and it can easily be adapted from a double-strand to a four-strand necklace as shown in the variation. The beads in this project are African batik bone beads. These beautiful beads are often sold strung temporarily on rafia.

before you begin

materials

6 m (19 ft) waxed ivory colour linen
    beading cord
27 x 10 mm (⅜ in) spotted batik bone beads
32 x 10 mm (⅜ in) striped batik bone beads
1 x Chinese coin with centre hole, 2.5 cm
    (1 in) in diameter

tools

Ruler or measuring tape
Scissors
Needle with large eye
T-pin
Cushion
Instant-bond glue
Small clothes peg or clamp

making the necklace

1 Cut the length of waxed linen into one 1 m (3 ft) and two 2.5 m (8 ft) lengths. Fold the two 2.5 m (8 ft) lengths in half, pinching them together with a 7.5 cm (3 in) loop in the middle (or large enough to fit over your coin and bead ending). Pinch the 1 m (3 ft) length together as well, with most of its length coming out to the top. Make an overhand knot (see page 21).

2 Thread the 1 m (3 ft) length onto the needle and use it to cover the loop with a buttonhole stitch (see page 21). When you have covered the entire loop, use the needle to weave your thread end back through the knot.

3 Bring all six ends of thread through a spotted bead and trim off the two short buttonhole-stitch ends. Separate the remaining four strands into two groups of two and make an overhand knot. Pull tight to the base of the spotted bead.

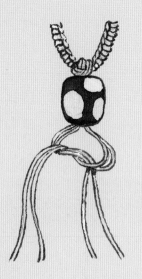

4 Use the T-pin and cushion to secure your work so you can keep a firm tension on the cords, then work the four strands in double half-hitch knots as shown in the instructions on page 21.

5 When the knotted strand is 4 cm (1½ in) long, separate it into two sets of two strands and make overhand knots as close to the macramé knots as possible. String 25 spotted beads on one set of two strands, then clamp it with a peg or clip while you thread 31 striped beads on the other. The outer strand of beads should be about 5 cm (2 in) longer. Make overhand knots after each of the last beads. Then make one overhand knot, tying all four strands together.

6 Using the shorter lengths of thread as cords two and three, carry on with 3.5 cm (1¼ in) of double half-hitch knots. Separate four strands into two groups of two and make an overhand knot. Add one spotted bead then make another overhand knot, as illustrated below, and 1 cm (⅜ in) more of double half-hitch knots.

7 Thread all four ends through a striped bead. Separate into two sets of two strands and make an overhand knot. Bring the four ends up through the hole in the coin. Bring two strands through one end of a spotted bead and two strands through the other end. Bring them both back down through the coin and make several knots around the base. Put a drop of glue on the knot. Let it dry and then trim the ends.

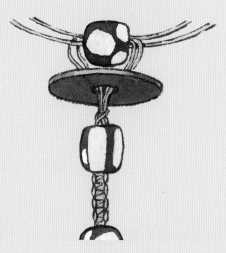

tips

❋ You can make a board to hold your macramé knots. Simply hammer nails into a piece of wood and then loop the tops of the threads around them.

❋ An alternative method is to stick a T-pin through the top overhand knot of your work and then into a firm cushion.

variation four-strand necklace

This necklace can be made in any length and it is a good
style to support heavier beads. This four-strand variation is
made in the same way as the main project, but each strand
is threaded individually instead of being grouped into two
strands. A variety of old and new striped and plain African
trade beads were used.

stepping stones
variation double-strand bracelet

This simple yet stunning bracelet combines sterling silver beads with labradorite stones, which give off a rainbow of opalescent colours. You could also try using grey or dark-coloured pearls, hematine (a manmade hematite), abalone shell beads, smoky quartz, or glass beads. Any of these will complement this colour scheme beautifully. Sterling silver beads are available in many shapes and sizes. Some are coated with an aged patina colour that will be 'worn' to a brighter silver in raised areas of the design. These look particularly beautiful with the stones mentioned here.

before you begin

materials

25 cm (10 in) beading wire

9 x 4 mm (³⁄₁₆ in) sterling silver beads

32 x 3 mm (⅛ in) cylinder cut silver beads

24 labradorite stones

2 crimp beads

1 toggle closure

tools

Flush wire cutters

Needle-nose pliers

Scissors

making the bracelet

1 Thread one end of the beading wire through a crimp bead, and then through a silver cylinder bead. Pass it through the ring end of the toggle closure and back through the silver bead and crimp bead. Crush the crimp bead, leaving a 2 cm (¾ in) tail on the short end of the beading wire to weave through the first few beads of stringing. String one silver cylinder bead on both wire ends.

2 Begin stringing as follows: three labradorite stones, two cylinder beads, one 4 mm (⅜ in) silver bead and two more cylinder beads. Repeat sequence seven times.

tips

* If you leave only a small loop of the beading wire at the top of the beads, attach the loop to a jump ring and then fasten the jump ring to the toggle closure.

* Other styles of closure can be attached to jewellery using the methods described in this project.

3 String three labradorite stones, two silver cylinders and one crimp bead through the other end of the toggle closure. Go back through the crimp bead and cylinder beads. Pull the beading wire so there is no slackness, but not so tight that it is rigid. Crush the crimp bead with the pliers. Weave the end of the beading wire through a few beads and trim the ends.

variation double-strand bracelet

Two strands can be attached to the same jump ring to make a
double-stranded bracelet or necklace. This bracelet is made with
colour-lined crystals and blue and lilac pearls. The two strands
were linked at each end with a crimp bead and another crystal
bead before being attached to the jump ring. Closures can be
bought with attachments for more strands.

simple charmers

To make the dazzling jewellery pieces in this section requires the simple beading techniques that you have already learned with some slightly more complex construction methods that provide delicate touches for added finesse.

The process of stringing beads on headpins and eyepins and then creating a loop in the wire is a skill that is essential for jewellery making. This technique is used to make the charms for the Charming Bracelet on pages 64–67, and the Bluebird Earrings on pages 52–55. Another method of constructing earrings is to use special beads with holes running through one tip, usually referred to as drop or dagger beads. You will find this method described in the Chalcedony Drop Earrings project on pages 56–59.

Simple bead weaving is demonstrated in the rings on pages 68–71 and pages 76–79. A delicate multi-strand starry necklace and a lariat also show new necklace designs and suggest some uses for the beaded beads shown in the following chapter.

bluebird earrings
variations vintage button earrings

Simple earrings can be made very quickly using headpins or eyepins. The earrings in this project are a little more complex because of the flower cap but look more impressive when finished. Here, vintage glass flowers and birds have been used, but there are many alternatives. Cabochons and buttons without shanks also work well. Elements from other old pieces of jewellery can also be incorporated into earring fronts using epoxy glue. Look out for old clip-on earrings. Remove the shanks with a pair of cutters and sand the back to provide a good base for the earring posts.

before you begin

materials

2 earring posts with stoppers
4 eyepins (plus extra for practice)
2 blue glass flowers, no smaller than
      6 mm (¼ in)
2 x 3 mm (⅛ in) pink rose montees
2 x 5 mm (³⁄₁₆ in) pink glass beads
2 glass bird charms

tools

Wire cutters
Epoxy glue
Needle-nose pliers
Toothpicks
Round-nose pliers

making the earrings

1 Mix a teaspoon of epoxy glue according to the maker's directions. Using a toothpick, apply a liberal dot to the centre of the flower front. Let the glue settle for a few seconds, then carefully place a rose montee on the glue. Leave it to dry while you continue.

2 Place the pink bead on your eyepin and then cut the end of the eyepin off so that about 1 cm (⅜ in) remains above the bead. You may need to try it a few times to get it right.

3 Place the tip of the wire end flush with the top of the round-nose pliers. Bend the end into a loop. Then turn the loop so it is up and facing away from you.

4 With the needle-nose pliers, grab the back of the loop just above the bead and pull it towards you. You should now have a nicely shaped loop. Hang the bird charm from one loop.

5 If the epoxy glue has set on the flower, you may begin work on the other side. Using another eyepin, make a loop in the other end that is large enough to fit around your earring post but not as large as your flower. Mix up some more epoxy glue and put a generous drop on the flower back. Place the loop and earring post in the glue and leave to dry.

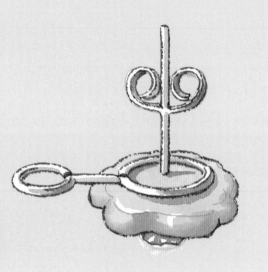

6 Open the loop hanging from the flower and fit your dangle on. Close the loop with pliers. Repeat for the second earring.

tips

✳ To open eyepins always move the end to one side with a pair of pliers rather than opening the circle.

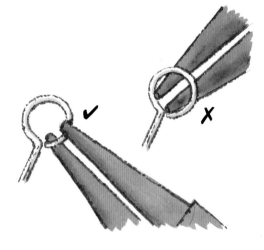

✳ When cutting wire, always restrain the cut end with fingers or fingertip to stop it flying away.

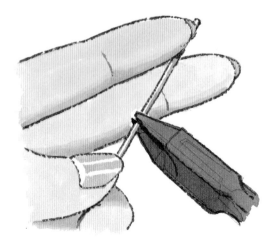

variations vintage button earrings

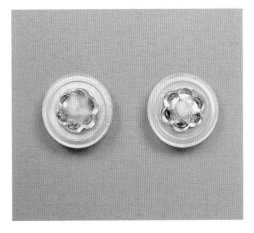

mother-of-pearl button earrings

A plain pair of vintage mother-of-pearl buttons have been dressed up with small glass flowers.

red star earrings

The Bakelite cog buttons at the top of these earrings inspired the colour choice for the other beads.

number button earrings

These have a funky asymmetrical look with their different numbers and lime-green flower bells. Use a more traditional button for a classic look.

flower button earrings

A charming pair of glass flower buttons with little beads stuck in the middle have made a wonderful pair of simple earrings.

chalcedony drop earrings
variation candy jade earrings

Dangling earrings of beads are very quick and easy to make. They can look as whimsical or as precious as you want. These earrings are made with tiny sterling silver beads and a beautiful faceted semi-precious drop stone. A 'drop' is any bead with a hole that runs horizontally through one end rather than top to bottom.

You can make an earring out of any kind of drop bead using a flexible wire or thread. The drop bead in this project is relatively heavy so beading wire was used. For a lighter bead a strong nylon thread will also work.

before you begin

materials

2 top-drilled, diamond-shaped, faceted,
    blue chalcedony stones
2 x 4 mm (³⁄₁₆ in) decorative, sterling
    silver beads
4 x 2 mm (¹⁄₁₆ in) rectangular, faceted sterling
    silver beads
24 charlottes or other seed beads
20 cm (8 in) fine beading wire
2 clam-shell bead tips
2 crimp beads
2 sterling silver earring wires

tools

Wire cutters
Pliers with a jaw wide enough to close clams
Needle-nose pliers or crimping pliers

making the earrings

1 Cut a 10 cm (4 in) length of wire with the wire cutters. Thread one end of the wire through a clam-shell bead tip, then through one large silver bead, three charlottes, one small silver bead, three more charlottes and then through the top of the drop stone.

2 Repeat the pattern on the other side of the loop, ending with both ends of the wire coming up through the final silver bead and the bead tip.

3 Put a crimp bead over both wire ends and pull the wires up so that the beads do not move on the wire, but not so tight that the wire is rigid. Hold it in this position while pushing the crimp bead to the base of the bead tip. Squeeze the crimp bead with pliers, and then clip any excess wire.

4 Shut the bead tip with the wide-jawed pliers and hook its end through the loop in the earring hooks. Close the loop with pliers. Repeat the steps for the second earring.

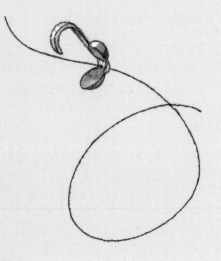

tips

✳ Crimping pliers are specially shaped to close crimping beads but a good pair of needle-nose pliers will also do the job.

✳ Use the flush side of the wire cutters to cut off any visible wire ends.

✳ Check that the clam-shell bead tip holds the drop stone facing forward rather than to the side of your head. This will depend on the orientation of the loop in your earring wire.

variation candy jade earrings

The drop stones in these earrings are made with candy jade, which is a recent innovation. It refers to jade stones that have been colour treated. These particular ones are an orange shade, but greens, blues and purples are also available. The colours look natural and include some striking variations.

starry nights
variation star earrings

The beaded stars used in this project are very easy to make (see pages 94–95 for directions). You can use them as charms on bracelets or necklaces, or adapt them to make earrings as in the variation shown on page 63. Here they adorn a simple string of tiny Thai silver beads and metallic-grey hematite stars to make a delicate necklace. Using different-sized seed beads can alter the size of the star, and the shape of the star can be changed by altering the number of seed beads in the points. A star with fewer beads on one side of a point than another will look more organic, like a starfish.

before you begin

materials

For the stars:

5 g (³⁄₁₆ oz) assorted 11° seed beads in grey,
     silver, black, white and burgundy

Grey nylon beading thread, size D

For the necklace:

1 x 40 cm (16 in) strand of 2 mm (¹⁄₁₆ in)
     Thai silver beads

1.2 m (47 in) beading wire, .010 diameter

1 clasp

2 jump rings

2 x 1 mm (¹⁄₁₆ in) crimp beads

5 g (³⁄₁₆ oz) 11° silver-lined grey seed beads

16 x 7 mm (¼ in) hematite stars

2 x 5 mm (³⁄₁₆ in) black crystals

tools

Size 12 sharps needle

Beeswax or thread conditioner

Crimping pliers or needle-nose pliers

Small clothes pegs or paper clips

Scissors

Liquid seam sealant

making the necklace

1 Begin by making eight beaded stars out of the 11° seed beads using the waxed nylon thread (see pages 94–95 for instructions). Make predominantly silver-coloured stars with a little black, grey, white and burgundy mixed in. One tip point of each star should have a loop of seven beads to hang it from the necklace.

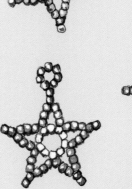

2 On the beading wire, string one jump ring and move it into the middle. Holding the wire ends together, string one 11° silver-lined seed bead and one crimp bead. Crush the crimp bead closed with the crimping pliers or needle-nose pliers.

3 Holding the two strands of wire together, string on 10 cm (4 in) of 11° silver-lined grey beads, and then one black crystal.

4 Clamp the outer string with the clip. On the inner strand, string ten silver beads, one hematite star, ten silver beads, one hematite star and five silver beads. String through the top bead on the loop of a beaded star.

5 Continue stringing the inner strand following the pattern of the necklace (see page 60), ending with a black crystal. Clamp the strand.

tip

✳ Although the shape of beaded stars can be changed by altering the number of seed beads in the points, a maximum of four is usually the best for stability.

6 The outer strand starts with five silver beads and one hematite star, then follows the pattern in Step 4, stringing five beaded stars at intervals as shown below. Bring the end through the same black crystal as the inner strand.

7 Working with both strands of wire together, string 10 cm (4 in) of 11° silver-lined grey beads, one crimp bead and one 11° bead. Bring the wire through a jump ring and back down through the 11° bead and the crimp bead. Crush the crimp bead and weave the ends through a few beads before trimming.

8 Open the loops in the jump rings and attach them to the closure before closing them with the needle-nose pliers.

variation star earrings

Beaded stars make wonderful earrings. They can be combined with other stones or hung in multiples from seed bead strands. Tiny stars, made from silver 15° beads (or smaller), look beautiful hung with old sterling silver charms.

charming bracelet
variation mixed charm bracelet

This project offers a colourful take on the traditional silver charm bracelet. Charms of vintage glass and plastic beads hang from a simple two-strand bracelet with a button closure. This style of bracelet can look dramatically different depending on your choice of bead colours and styles. Delicate beaded beads and glass buttons in dark colours provide a sophisticated look, while charms of bright vintage plastics make an unusual and more contemporary style of bracelet. You can use silver charms from old charm bracelets, combining them with blue and violet beads, or include only a few charms for a simpler look.

To establish bracelet size, follow the directions for the Fairy Chain Bracelet on page 32.

before you begin

materials

8 headpins
8 eyepins
90 x 10° tri-cut orange beads
1 x 18 mm (¾ in) button with shank
1 m (39 in) fishing line
8 red glass stars
10 x 6° white hearts (red glass with
    a white core)
8 x 5 mm (³⁄₁₆ in) red glass beads
42 x 6° striped beads
10 purple crystal beads

tools

Needle-nose pliers
Round-nose pliers
Wire cutters
Scissors
Small clothes peg or clamp

making the bracelet

1 This bracelet has eight charms made from combinations of beads hanging from headpins and eyepins. Make them up before you begin stringing the bracelet. To make a charm, place a star bead on a headpin and then cut off the end of the pin so that you have about 1 cm (⅜ in) above the star. This measurement will vary depending on the circumference of the pliers where you wrap the wire (in step 2). You may need to try it a few times to get it right.

2 Place the tip of the wire end flush with the top of the round-nose pliers at their smallest point. Bend the end into a loop. (See page 53 for illustrations.)

3 Turn the loop so it is up and facing away from you. Using your needle-nose pliers, grab the back of the loop just above the bead and pull it towards you to make a nicely shaped loop.

4 Place one striped bead, one 6° white heart and one purple crystal on an eyepin. Cut the wire 1 cm (⅜ in) above the last bead and bend into a loop as before. Open the headpin with the star bead by moving the loop sideways with your pliers and slip it onto the eyepin with three beads. Close the loop. Make up eight charms in this manner.

5 In the middle of your length of fishing line, thread enough seed beads to form a loop large enough to fit over the button. String one purple crystal, one striped bead, and one purple crystal onto both ends of the fishing line.

6 Clamp one side of the fishing line with a clip and on the other string three seed beads, one striped bead, one charm, one striped bead, three seed beads, one striped bead, one large red bead and one striped bead. Repeat three more times and then string three seed beads. Secure with a clamp while you thread the other side.

7 The second strand begins with three seed beads, then one striped bead, one large red bead, one striped bead, three seed beads, one striped bead, one charm, one striped bead and three seed beads. Repeat three more times.

8 Bring the two ends together and make a three-bead grouping. String one white heart, one striped bead, one white heart. If you want your bracelet to be larger, you could use longer beads here to create more length.

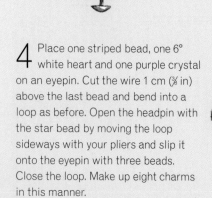

9 Attach the button to the bracelet. Thread five seed beads onto each strand. Bring one strand through each side of the button shank. Bring each strand back down through the five seed beads and make a double knot. Thread both ends through the first bead in your three-bead grouping and make a double-knot. Repeat this for each bead in the grouping and then push the thread through the first 2 cm (¾ in) of beads on each strand.

10 Cut the ends and add a drop of instant-bond glue to one of the knots in the bead grouping.

tips

* If the holes of the charms are so large that they slide along the seed beads you may want to put slightly larger stopper beads on either side of them.

* Open eyepins by moving the loop to one side rather than opening the circle (see page 54).

* Be careful when cutting wire. Hold the end to be cut to stop it flying away (see page 54).

* The weight of the dangles can cause the bracelet to hang under your palm. Do not make it too loose or the dangles will get in the way. You can counterbalance your bracelet by selecting a heavy button and hanging a heavy charm from your button loop.

* Be careful to close the loops at the top of your charms fully so that they do not fall off your fishing line.

variation mixed charm bracelet

This variation has many charms in bright summer colours and themes. Some of the charms include an extra dangle hanging from the end for even more movement. Vintage and new glass beads, such as the birds and flowers, were combined with vintage Lucite spotted beads.

bow tie band ring
variations coordinating beaded ring and bracelet

The weave pattern used in this project stretches a little and looks like a bow tie when it is on your finger. The slight stretch makes it a useful design when you are making a ring for someone else's finger and you do not know their size. Beaded rings are very quick to make up. Any woven circle of beads can be a ring and it can be fun to experiment with different beads, colours and weave patterns, and to invent new designs. It is simple to expand your designs to make a matching bracelet.

before you begin

materials

50 x 12° ruby iris charlottes (Bead A)
20 x 4 mm (³⁄₁₆ in) faceted, pink crystal beads
    (Bead B)
10 x 11° pink-lined beads (Bead C)
Pink nylon beading thread, size D

tools

Beeswax
Size 12 sharps needle
Scissors
Needle-nose pliers

making the ring

1 This ring is made up of a simple woven circle with five pattern repeats. Work with doubled waxed thread and maintain good tension so that your finished ring will not be floppy. Follow the thread path illustrated, adding the beads in number order. Use the following beads:

Bead A: 1–4, 7–9, 11–14, 17–19
Bead B: 5, 10, 15, 20
Bead C: 6, 16

After bead 20, thread through beads 3 and 5 to 13 again to start the next sequence with a B bead.

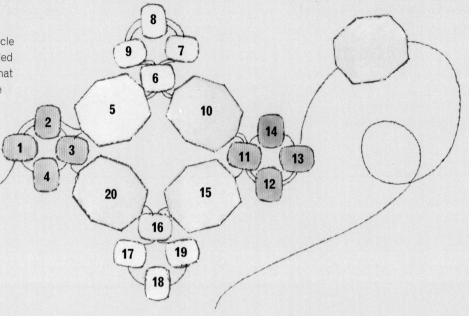

2 Repeat the sequence four times. For your fifth and final sequence, you will join the ends together. To do this, work through beads 1 to 4 instead of adding beads 11 to 14 in the sequence.

3 To finish, make a knot and weave in the ends (see page 20).

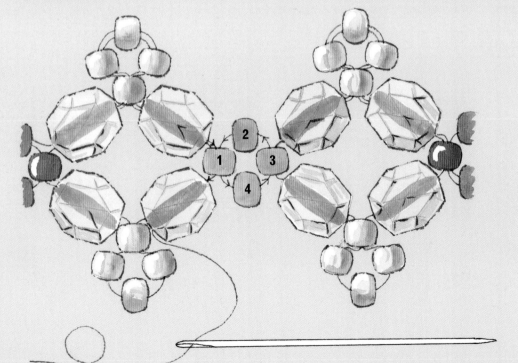

tips

✳ Needle-nose pliers can help to coax the needle through beads that are full of threads.

✳ Using these exact beads will give you a ring to fit a medium-sized ring finger. The weave allows the ring to stretch a little bit. Choosing larger seed beads or increasing the number of beads in the pattern will make a larger ring.

variations coordinating beaded ring and bracelet

This ring was made using the same pattern but instead of using just one bead in positions 2 and 4, three beads are used, but worked as one. In this case, the central bead of the three is in colour C. This makes the ring quite a lot larger. Two beads could have been used instead to provide a smaller increase in size. The bracelet was made to match. The pattern was repeated 11 times and the clasp was created in the same way as with the Splash Lariat necklace on pages 72–74.

A lariat is a necklace that fastens with a tie at the front. This design features a loop through which you feed the opposite end. Both ends have heavy beads so that the necklace stays fastened. The 'candy cage' is the name for the playful beaded bead that dangles in front. It has a hollow centre that you can leave empty or put a glass bead inside, left free to jingle. This necklace is made of a combination of heishi beads and glass rondelles but many variations are possible depending on the beads you choose.

splash lariat
variation double-stranded pearl lariat

before you begin

materials

For the candy cage:

30 x 8° pale yellow seed beads (Bead A)

10 x 4 mm (³⁄₁₆ in) turquoise glass beads (Bead B)

5 x 4 mm (³⁄₁₆ in) pink glass beads (Bead C)

Nylon beading thread

For the lariat:

1.5 m (5 ft) fishing line, 5.4 kg (12 lb) test weight

2 x 13 mm (½ in) glass flower beads (or other significant end bead)

8 x 7 mm (¼ in) ruby-red stone or glass rondelles

2 x 13 mm (½ in) spotted glass beads

13 x 7 mm (¼ in) turquoise heishi

1 x 41 cm (16 in) strand of 5 mm (³⁄₁₆ in) heishi in watermelon Lucite

4 x 4 mm (³⁄₁₆ in) pink glass beads

3 x 4 mm (³⁄₁₆ in) turquoise glass beads

5 g (³⁄₁₆ oz) 8° pale yellow seed beads

tools

Size 12 sharps needle

Beeswax or thread conditioner

Scissors

Needle-nose pliers

Instant-bond glue

Pliers

Small clothes peg or clamp

making the necklace

1 Make a candy cage bead following the directions on pages 92–93. When you have finished, thread the fishing line through bead C of your candy cage, making sure that both lengths are equal.

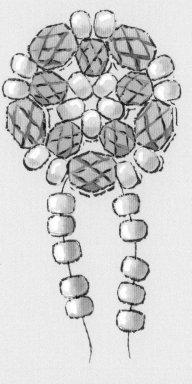

2 Thread five 8° beads on to each end then make a bead grouping. Put both thread ends through one 5 mm (³⁄₁₆ in) heishi, one 7 mm (¼ in) rondelle, one spotted glass bead, one 5 mm (³⁄₁₆ in) heishi, one 7 mm (¼ in) heishi, one 5mm (³⁄₁₆ in) heishi and one 8° bead. If the spotted glass bead has a large hole, you may want to fill it up with seed beads that fit inside it, so that it does not move too much on the line.

3 Tie a knot, then working with the two strands apart again, string enough seed beads onto each end of the thread to create a loop just big enough for your biggest bead, on the other end, to fit through.

4 String both ends together through an 8° bead, tie another knot and begin working the beading pattern illustrated below, bringing both ends through all beads. You may design your own sequence as long as you plan your end after 53 cm (21 in).

5 Repeat the bead sequence five and a half times and then add the second large glass bead, followed by one 7 mm (¼ in) rondelle and one 5 mm (³⁄₁₆ in) heishi.

6 Now work the two ends separately to different lengths. On the first, longer strand, thread eleven 8° beads, one pink 4 mm (³⁄₁₆ in) glass bead, one flower and one 8° bead. Take the fishing line back up through the flower, make a knot, then up through the glass bead, make a knot, up through the seed beads, knot again, and then weave in the ends (see page 20). Put a drop of instant-bond glue on the knots.

7 Repeat the process for the shorter strand, using only six 8° beads to start. Trim the fishing line ends. Wear the necklace by feeding the flowers and the big glass bead through the opposite loop.

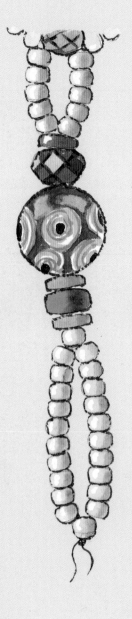

tips

❋ Try on the lariat before making the knots, to check that you are happy with the length of the closure and hanging ends.

❋ Use small clothes pegs or clamps to hold the beads on the line while testing the design.

variation double-stranded pearl lariat

To create a weightier looking necklace, string the two ends separately throughout the necklace instead of working them together after creating the loop closure. This will give you a two-strand lariat. If you want an even fuller look, make the lariat long enough to wrap around your neck twice. The ends can be as long as you like but stagger them so that all the ending beads are visible. You may finish with one heavy bead or a small cluster of lighter beads, but it is important to create some weight at the end of the strands to support the necklace closure and ensure the lariat hangs nicely.

black beauty ring

variations blue glass ring and seed bead rings

This open chain-shaped weave lends itself to an embellished floral front. Although this weave pattern does not stretch much, adding more links in the 'chain' or making a larger flower can increase the size. You can work this simple chain to the length needed for a necklace or bracelet as well. Just add a toggle closure. If you are going to work the chain up for a larger piece of jewellery, consider enlarging the beads used, or hanging dangles from the beaded loops.

before you begin

materials

22 x 11˚ matt-black beads (Bead A)

44 x 11˚ silver-lined transparent smoke beads
  (Bead B)

24 x 8˚ silver-lined transparent smoke beads
  (Bead C)

8 x 4 mm (³⁄₁₆ in) black faceted crystals

1 x 4 mm (³⁄₁₆ in) rose montee
  (you can substitute another small bead)

Black nylon beading thread, size D

tools

Needle-nose pliers

Size 12 sharps needle

Beeswax or thread conditioner

Scissors

making the ring

1 Work with doubled waxed thread and maintain a firm
  tension so that your finished ring will not be floppy.
Follow the sequence in the illustration below using the
following beads:

Bead A: beads 1, 2, 6, 7, 14, 15
Bead B: beads 3, 5, 8, 10, 11, 13, 16, 18
Bead C: beads 4, 9, 12, 17

After bead 10, thread through beads 1 to 7 again, to start
the next sequence with a B bead.

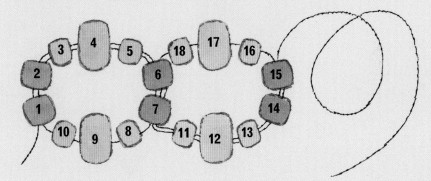

2 Continue this sequence approximately ten times, or
  until the ends just about meet when wrapped around
your finger. You may need to make the final circle slightly
larger to accommodate finger size. To do this, add extra
B beads as shown in the illustration below.

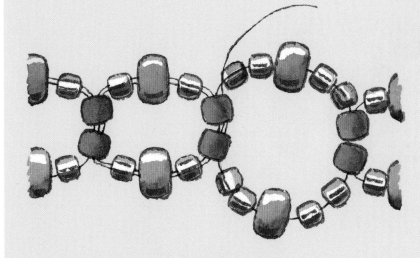

3 Embellish the centre of the ring by weaving through the beads of the final circle, and adding the black faceted crystals and smaller smoke beads as illustrated below. You could make more petals if you wish.

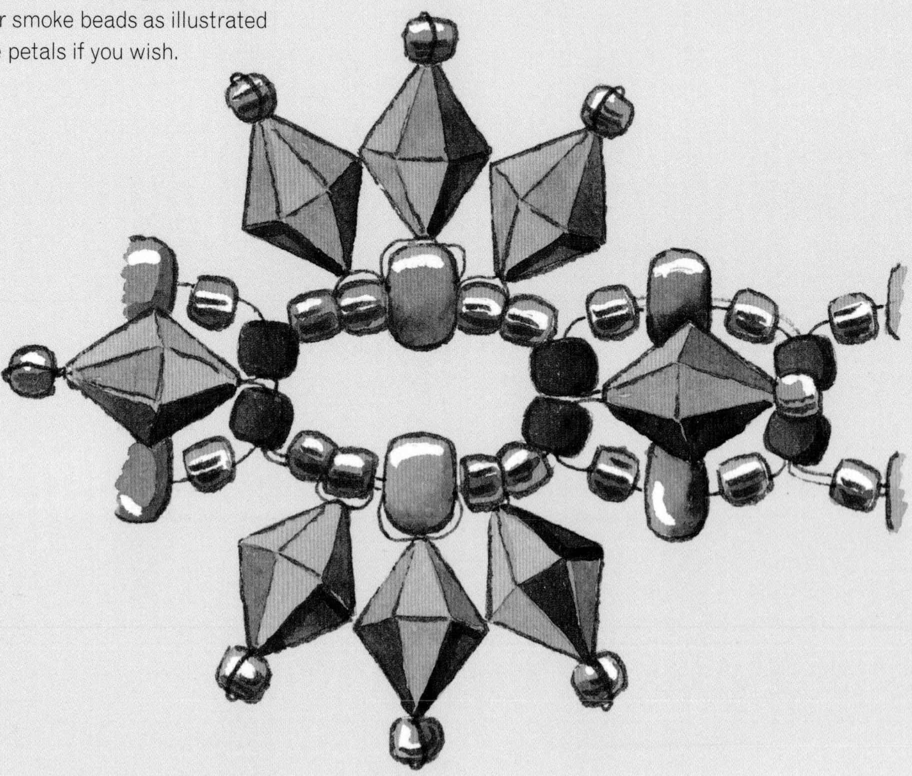

4 Add the rose montee by working the thread between the two vertical beads on either side of the flower as shown in the illustration below. Weave in the threads to finish (see page 20).

tips

✳ The final circle in the pattern is where the size of the ring is determined. You can add more or fewer beads as required to make the ring larger or smaller.

✳ Put embellishments on the final circle if it differs in size from the rest of the pattern. They will hide it from view while the uniform patterns will be on show.

variations blue glass ring and seed bead rings

blue glass ring

This blue ring is made in the same way as the main project but fewer beads have been used for the petals and there is no central bead in the flower detail.

narrow seed bead ring

This ring follows the same pattern as the ring in the main project, but uses only seed beads of one size and it has no flower focal point. It makes a great pattern to start children bead weaving. Experiment by substituting differently coloured or shaped beads into the basic pattern.

seed bead ring

The weaving pattern in this ring is very simple to master. Follow the instructions for right-angle weave (see page 22) using contrasting colours for the vertical and horizontal beads. The example uses light blue cylinder beads for the vertical and matt opaque-blue iridescent beads along the horizontal. Three rounds are completed and then the blue beads are woven into the gaps along the upper and lower edges.

weaving your own magic

This chapter introduces you to basic bead weaving techniques. By stitching small beads together you can create many elements, such as beaded beads and buttons, stars and starfish, flowers and leaves, that you can incorporate into your jewellery. Bead weaving can also form an entire piece of jewellery as demonstrated in the Beaded Button Earrings on page 91.

If you incorporate a combination of seed beads and small glass and metal beads in your beaded beads, the result will be a stunning array of colour, reflections and glints of light. These beaded beads look wonderful strung together or used as charms in combination with other beads.

Many of the elements shown in this chapter have been used in projects in other parts of the book. Look at the Splash Lariat necklace on pages 72–75 to see a variation of the candy cage bead or see the Silver Seeds project on pages 114–117 for a leafy variation of the beaded flower charm.

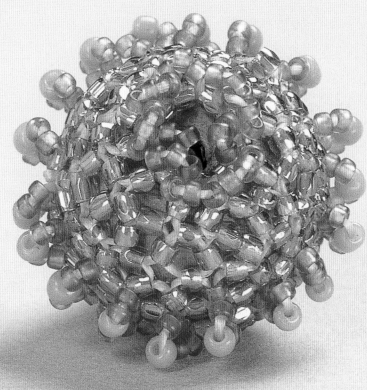

beaded bead
variations embellished beaded beads

Larger beads can be created with seed beads in many different ways. The most common method is to weave small beads around a larger base bead. To make a pendant for a necklace, use a glass bead at the core to give it some weight. For earrings, a light wood or plastic core bead is more suitable. Remember when choosing your core bead that the final size will be much larger once you have woven the covering. You can use seed beads of all sizes and shapes to cover a bead. On larger beads, small beads in glass, stone or metal can also be used.

before you begin

materials

1 x 10 mm (⅜ in) core bead
5 g (³⁄₁₆ oz) matt red seed beads
10 cm (4 in) 18-gauge copper wire
Red nylon beading thread, size D

tools

Scissors
Size 12 sharps needle
Beeswax or thread conditioner
Wire cutters
Round-nose pliers

making the beaded bead

1 To begin the bead, make a loop of seed beads: thread eight beads, leaving a 6 cm (2⅜ in) tail. Tie a knot so the beads form a circle and bring your needle through the first two or three beads.

2 Work a right-angle weave (see page 22) with the core bead strung on a wire. This will hold the beads on to begin with and help your grip. You will discard the wire when the bead is finished. Using the pliers, bend a loop into one end of the wire. Place the woven circle of beads on the wire through the centre, and then place the core bead on. With your pliers make another loop and cut the wire. The wire should fit snugly so that the work does not move around.

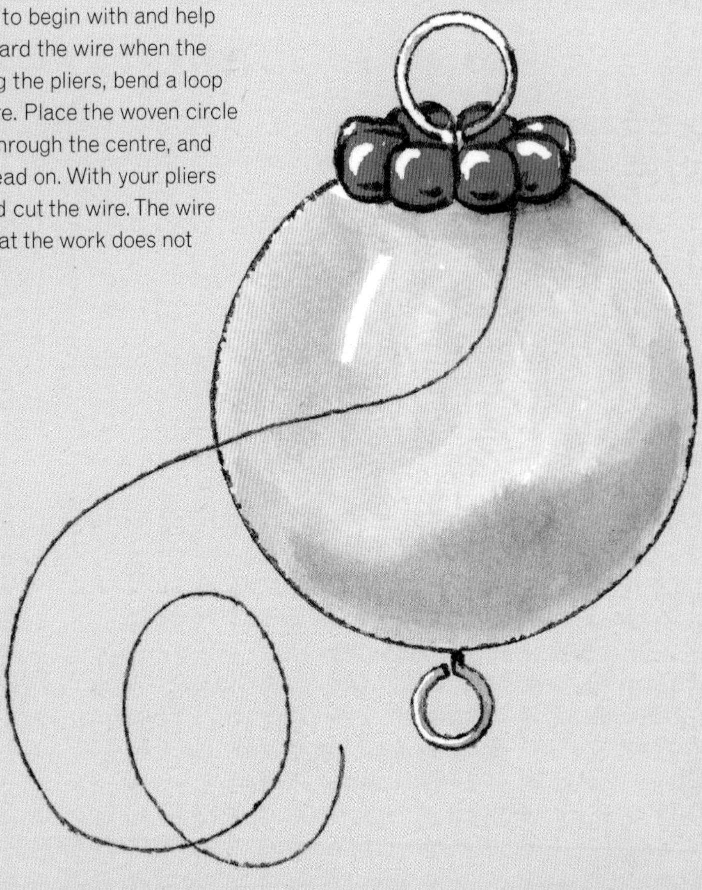

3 Thread on three beads, then take the needle back through beads A, 1, 2, 3 and then through bead B.

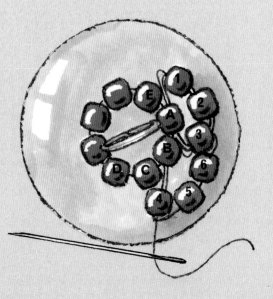

4 Thread on three beads again. If you were not increasing you would just add two beads. However, as the circumference of your core bead widens, you need to increase. Go back through bead 3, bead B, and come out through bead 4.

5 Add two beads (you are only increasing at every other bead) then go through bead C and back through bead 4. Add two more beads before coming out through bead D.

6 Continue weaving beads alternating adding three (an increase) and two beads with every other group. To complete the circle the last weave will join the ends together adding one bead between. Bring the needle through E and 1 and out through bead 2 to begin the next round. Bead 2 will become the base to which you add the first three beads of your next round.

7 Continue beading, adding increases when the beads are becoming too snug around your core bead. This is not very precise because it depends on the size and shape of your seed beads and core bead. When you have gone past the middle of your core bead, you will need to decrease.

8 To decrease, skip over a bead in the outer circle. Towards the end of the core bead, you will need to decrease drastically so that you end with your needle going through eight beads. Weave in the ends (see page 20) and remove your bead from the wire.

tips

✷ It may be helpful to weave a band of straightforward right-angle weave before you begin, to familiarize yourself with the pattern of the weave. A band of four rows in an 11° bead or a small glass bead can make a simple bracelet.

✷ If there are gaps in the beading due to uneven increasing and decreasing, these can easily be hidden by weaving beads into them or embellishing when the bead is complete.

✷ You can use a variety of differently sized, shaped or coloured seed beads on the same core bead since the increasing and decreasing pattern is obvious while making the bead.

embellishing bead weaving

You can embellish any woven beadwork, including beaded buttons and beads, as well as flat stitches. Embellishing is simply adding beads to the surface of the design that are not integral to the structure of the weave. A wide variety of beads and patterns can be used to create different looks: small or big loops, pyramid edging, bugle beads to make spikes, faceted beads to add sparkle and drops or daggers to create bumps. The possibilities are endless.

five-bead loop

This embellishment uses the same principle as the three-bead loop but smaller beads may be used.

three-bead loop

Here the bead weaving is embellished by stitching through a base bead, adding three beads, and going back through the base bead in the same direction as the first time, creating a loop of beads around the base bead. This can be done randomly over the surface of a bead or it can be done to every bead in one or more rows for a denser look.

points

Spiky loops can be created by making a point with a small bead on top then stringing through the second-to-last bead twice as shown in the illustration. To accentuate the spiky shape, make the loops between beads rather than on top of them, although this could create an interesting look too.

pearls

Here, a tiny button-shaped pearl is used in place of small beads.
Try other interestingly shaped small beads as well.

bugle-bead spikes

Bugle beads used in place of seed beads will stick straight up. Do
not use bugle beads longer than 8 mm (⁵⁄₁₆ in), as the work may be
too vulnerable to snagging.

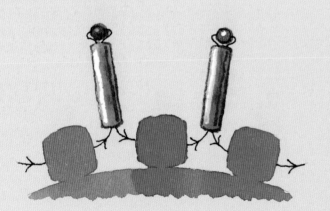

tips

✻ Thread colour may show
between beads so try to match
it to the colour of the piece that
you are embellishing.

✻ Bead loops can be as large as
you like but choose an odd
number of beads.

✻ Embellishing is more
vulnerable to wear and tear
because it sticks out,
particularly on items such as
beads on a charm bracelet. If
it is likely to receive a lot of
wear, reinforce the beads with
a second round of thread. If it is
possible to use a doubled
thread, do so.

variations embellished beaded beads

These four beads have been embellished in a variety of styles. The large pink and gold bead has loops of pink seed beads around the top and middle. The large pink and red bead, and the small orange bead have different-coloured beads randomly placed in the weaving. The burgundy bead has been covered with spots of red glass beads.

There are many different ways to use beaded buttons. They make a wonderful closure for a special necklace or bracelet. The button can be worn at the back of the necklace or it can become a focal point at the centre of the front or worn to one side. Add an embellished button to the top of a bead-woven ring, or make them into earrings by including a loop of beads at the top of the button instead of the back. They are also a great way to test bead combinations before you embark on a larger project.

beaded button
variation beaded button earrings

before you begin

materials

1 button, 15 mm (⅝ in) in diameter. The button
   used in this example is 2.5 mm (⅛ in) thick
   at its widest point and has no ridges
5 g (³⁄₁₆ oz) 14˚ seed beads in matt dusty pink
5 g (³⁄₁₆ oz) 12˚ charlottes in iridescent purple
Pink and black nylon beading thread, size D

tools

Beeswax or thread conditioner
Scissors
Size 12 or 13 sharps needle
Needle-nose pliers

making the beaded button

1 Thread the needle with a long piece of conditioned pink nylon thread. Working with a single thread, string three charlotte beads and slide them 15 cm (6 in) from the end.

2 Tie the beads into a ring using a square knot (see page 21), and then pass the needle back through the first bead (bead number 1 in the diagram below). Follow the method for Peyote Stitch on page 22, working in circular rounds rather than rows. For round 2 pick up two beads in each space. When you get to the end of a round, pass the needle through the first bead of the previous round and the first two of the round that you are on.

3 Continue as in the diagram, increasing to 12 beads in round 4. Change to the charlottes for rounds 6 and 7. Return to the 14° beads and increase to 24 beads in round 8.

tips

✳ If you wish to use a larger button, continue increasing with circular peyote at regular intervals, making sure it remains flat, until the disk is slightly larger than your button size. Then begin to make decreases. Observing the distance between beads will guide you in deciding when to make increases and decreases.

✳ Do not choose beads with tiny holes because the needle and thread will need to make repeated passes through them.

✳ If you change colours and pattern beginning at round 12 you can make double-sided earrings to hang from a hoop.

✳ Round seed beads make a flatter, more even circular peyote than cylinder-shaped ones.

✳ Beaded buttons can be used to fasten a garment, but care must be taken when washing. Use a safety pin attached to the wrong side of the garment so you can remove the buttons before cleaning.

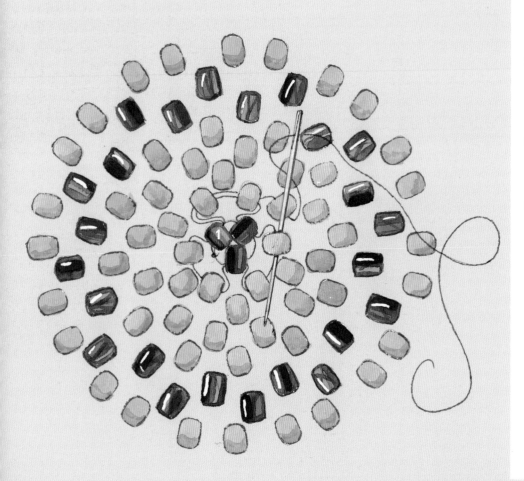

4 Continue working circular peyote over the 24 beads for three more rounds so that you are not increasing or decreasing. At round 12: decrease to 16 beads. Go through the first bead in round 11, pick up a new bead, go into the next bead in round 11, pick up a new bead and then go through two beads in round 11. Repeat until the round is complete and there are 16 beads in total. Pull the thread to maintain a tight tension.

5 At round 13, insert the button, then maintain 16 beads until round 17, using a tight tension. At round 17, decrease every other bead until there are eight beads.

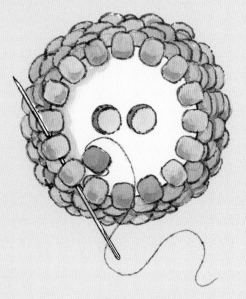

6 Round 18: work circular peyote over the eight beads. Round 19: decrease every other bead to a total of four beads. Round 20: go back with your needle through the last four beads.

7 Make a button shank or earring loop with seven beads. Embellish rounds 6 and 7 by adding three charlottes to each bead on the button. Weave in the ends to finish (see page 20).

variations beaded button earrings

Simple earrings can be made with plain or embellished button shapes by attaching earring wires to a beaded loop at the top of the covered button.

candy cage bead
variation iridescent candy cage beads

This is the type of bead that hangs from the Splash Lariat necklace on pages 72–75. You can weave it in many combinations and embellish it in the same way as the beaded beads on pages 85–87. The size and especially the shape of the beads you use to make the candy cage will affect the finished design. If larger beads are used you may need to switch to a larger beading thread material, such as clear fishing line, or you may need to make many more passes of the thread and needle. The aim is to fill up the bead holes with thread. This will prevent the candy cage bead from being floppy.

before you begin

materials
30 x 8° yellow beads (Bead A)
10 x 4 mm (³⁄₁₆ in) turquoise glass beads (Bead B)
5 x 4 mm (³⁄₁₆ in) pink glass beads (Bead C)
Neutral-coloured nylon beading thread, size D

tools
Size 12 sharps needle
Beeswax or thread conditioner
Scissors
Needle-nose pliers

making the candy cage bead

1 Working with waxed doubled thread, make a loop of five 8° beads, tie a knot and bring the thread out of the next bead. This becomes bead number 1. Follow the thread path in the illustration below using the following beads:

Bead A: beads 1–5, 7, 9, 11, 13, 16, 18, 19, 21, 23, 25
Bead B: beads 6, 10, 14, 15, 22
Bead C: beads 8, 12, 17, 20, 24

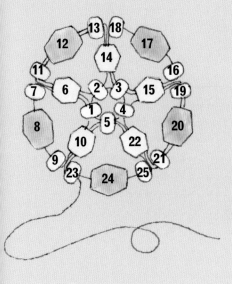

2 When you have completed the first medallion, bring your thread through all the beads a second time to strengthen the structure. Knot the thread, weave in the ends (see page 20) and trim them off.

3 Begin the other side of the candy cage by making a loop of five A beads. Add one bead B, one bead A and then go through one of the outside C beads from your first medallion. Add one bead A, one bead B and then go into the second bead of your five-bead loop. Repeat this sequence, joining all the C beads from the first medallion as you create your second medallion.

4 Reinforce the structure by threading through the beads again where needed, to create a firm bead. Weave in the ends (see page 20) and trim them off.

tips

❊ Do not choose beads with small holes to make your candy cage, because the needle needs to pass through some of them many times, particularly Bead C.

❊ Fill the candy cage holes with thread to make a firm bead.

variation iridescent candy cage beads

These two candy cages demonstrate the difference that the choice of bead makes. Both are made with iridescent 4 mm (³⁄₁₆ in) cube beads, but one uses coloured clear glass while the other is predominantly iridescent matt purple. The second bead also uses cube beads in the centre of the cage, which has given it a rounder shape.

beaded star

Beaded stars are wonderful for embellishing jewellery. Make them with size 6° or 8° seed beads and small crystals for sizeable charms or use tiny micro seed beads for delicate stars to hang from earrings. Experiment with different colour combinations and try mixing bead sizes within the star.

It is important to complete the second round of threading. It takes longer, but filling in the holes of the beads with thread will add strength and prevent floppy stars. These stars are so attractive that they may end up in many of your creations.

before you begin

materials

30 x 11° seed beads in black (Bead A)
10 x 11° seed beads in white (Bead B)
Neutral-coloured nylon beading thread, size D

tools

Size 12 sharps needle
Wax or thread conditioner
Needle-nose pliers
Liquid seam sealant

making the beaded star

1 Working with doubled waxed thread, string ten beads, alternating the colours. Make a double knot between the first and tenth bead leaving a 10 cm (4 in) tail. Bring your needle back through all the beads once, and then bring your thread out through the first bead.

3 Repeat step 2 for each of the five points in the star. Reinforce the entire star by repeating the thread path once. Put a drop of seam sealant on the thread and then trim the end.

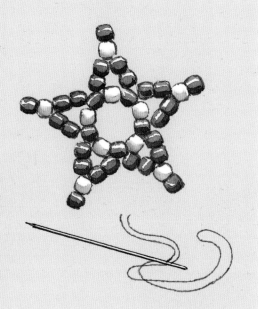

2 Following the numbered thread path below, string two A beads, one B bead, and one A bead. Bring your needle back through bead B and add two more A beads. Then bring your needle out through bead 7.

4 Thread the tail of the thread onto the needle and weave in the end (see page 20). Put a drop of seam sealant on the end and trim.

tip

✳ You can experiment with bead shape, size and colour but you can also vary the number of beads that go towards making the point and tip. A star can have three beads instead of two in the point and three beads instead of one in the tips. Alternatively, a star could have six beads in the tips.

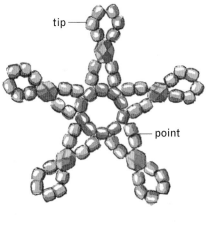

tip

point

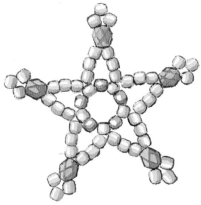

beaded flower charm
variation fuchsia flower bracelet

There are many uses for this simple charm. It expands the five-repeat circular formation of the Beaded Star (see pages 94–95) into a more substantial design. The inner circle of the flower remains rigid because the thread passes through the central beads many times. This provides many options for its use. It can become a charm for a necklace, bracelet or earrings. Alternatively, it can be left with no loop and sewn as an embellishment to a piece of bead weaving, such as a simple bracelet or ring. You could also combine it with a beaded button to make a brooch or a closure for a bracelet, as demonstrated in the variation on page 99.

before you begin

materials

65 x 11° brown-lined clear green beads
   (Bead A)

10 x 2.2 mm (1/16 in) twisted-hex bronze
   beads (Bead B)

50 x 11° green-bronze tri-cuts (Bead C)

30 x 11° silver-lined lime beads (Bead D)

Brown nylon beading thread, size D

tools

Size 13 sharps needle

Needle-nose pliers

Beeswax or thread conditioner

Liquid seam sealant

making the beaded flower charm

1 Working with a single, conditioned thread, leave a 6 cm (2⅜ in) tail and thread a stopper bead on your work (see page 9). You will take this off later but it helps to maintain tension while you are working. Begin with one twisted-hex bronze bead followed by 12 A beads. Go back through beads 3 and 4, and add one more bead A. Repeat this sequence a total of five times.

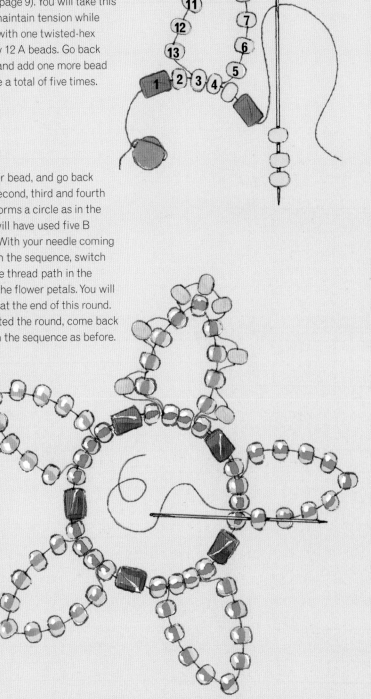

2 Remove the stopper bead, and go back through the first, second, third and fourth bead so that the work forms a circle as in the illustration below. You will have used five B beads and 65 A beads. With your needle coming out of the fourth bead in the sequence, switch to bead C and follow the thread path in the illustration for each of the flower petals. You will have added 35 C beads at the end of this round. When you have completed the round, come back out of the first bead 4 in the sequence as before.

3 Switch to bead D and repeat the thread path illustrated below for each of the petals. The petals will begin to cup slightly but this is fine. You will add 30 D beads over the course of this round. Again, bring your thread out of the fourth bead in the first petal.

5 For the fifth and final petal start the sequence as in step four but half way round when you have threaded on bead C on top of bead B, use 11 C beads to create the loop from which to hang the flower. Go around your loop twice, then complete the sequence in step four with the final three C beads. Weave your thread end back into your petal using seam sealant before you snip the end of the thread.

tips

✳ Begin beading with a single thread to make sure that you do not fill up holes before you have come to the end of the weaving pattern. However, be careful to maintain a good tension so that the beaded flower does not become floppy.

✳ Switch to waxed, doubled thread towards the end of the project if there is still space that needs filling in the holes.

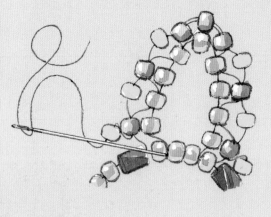

4 Using three D beads, one bead B, one bead C and three more D beads, repeat the sequence illustrated below, for four of the five petals.

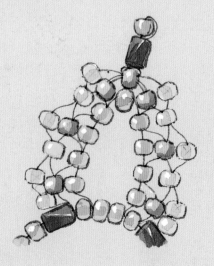

variation
fuchsia flower bracelet

The flower charm can make a wonderful closure if it is teamed with an unusually shaped button that will fit through the centre of the flower and hold fast when it lays flat. A star was used here but toggle shapes will also work.

show stoppers

Larger beaded pieces make wonderful decorative items, either as focal points for your jewellery or as stand-alone objects. The complexity of the pieces in this final section suggests sophistication. Jewellery pieces such as these are not readily available to buy. They are clearly handcrafted works of art.

Continuing with the techniques of bead weaving learned in the last section, a pair of beaded beads are transformed into thistle tassels for a pair of unusual earrings (see pages 102–105). There are also two tassel necklaces in this section: Autumn Fire (see pages 108–113) uses a stunning handmade focal bead and woven fringes while the second necklace, Tickled Pink Tassel (see pages 118–121), shows how to build and embellish a tassel with seed beads. These pieces, including many others, will really stop people in their tracks. Expect compliments!

thistle-bead earrings

variation thistle-bead iridescent danglers

Beaded beads make dramatic earrings because they can be embellished in so many ways. Adding a fringe, frills or spots of contrasting beads will result in a surface encrusted with colour, light and texture. Earrings are the perfect place to include precious pearls or other special beads, and those in this project feature a beautiful gold pearl drop at the bottom. Although small 14° beads have been used, larger beads up to 11°, such as those that appear in the variation, also look good and work up quickly.

before you begin

materials

2 x 10 mm (⅜ in) wood or plastic beads
   to cover
2 earring wires
2 headpins
5 g (³⁄₁₆ oz) 14° matt olive-green beads
5 g (³⁄₁₆ oz) 14° chocolate-bronze beads
35 x 12° tri-cuts in iridescent olive
2 x 5 mm (³⁄₁₆ in) gold pearls
2 x 3 mm (⅛ in) bronze beads
Grey nylon beading thread, size 0

tools

Round-nose pliers
Needle-nose pliers
Wire cutters
10 cm (4 in) 18-gauge copper wire
Size 15 beading needle
Scissors
Beeswax or thread conditioner

making the earrings

1 Following the instructions for beading a bead (see pages 82–84), weave a cover for your core bead using the 14° matt olive-green beads with the occasional tri-cut woven in to create a contrast in the colour and texture. Use the copper wire to secure the bead as you work.

2 Embellish the base of the bead with a fringe by working through 16 beads at the bottom of your beaded bead. Through each bead, string four matt olive beads, one tri-cut and one matt olive bead, then take the thread back up through the tri-cut and four olive beads, and out through the other side of the base bead that you began your fringe on.

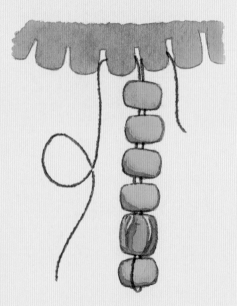

3 To make the strand that holds the pearl, start from the centre bottom of the bead, and create a strand of five matt olive beads, one tri-cut, the pearl, one tri-cut and then go back up through the pearl and the other beads.

4 To create the ruff around the bottom fringe, embellish with three 14° bronze beads through the beads around the outside edge of the fringe.

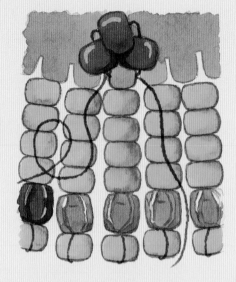

5 Create the ruff around the top of the bead by working through the ring of eight beads in the same manner.

6 Thread the headpin through your beaded bead and then through your 3 mm (⅛ in) bronze bead, which should nestle within the ruff.

7 Bend a loop at the top of the eyepin (see page 53) and hang it from the earring wire. Make a second earring to match.

tips

✳ To make the earrings identical, it may be easier to work each step on both earrings before moving on to the next step.

✳ Be sure not to pull the thread too taut while making the fringe or they will stick out at strange angles rather than hanging down neatly. The frill around the bottom will help to hold the fringes down.

✳ If you find the seed beads covering the core bead are filled with thread when you go to embellish it, you can use the thread between beads to anchor your embellishments instead.

✳ If it becomes difficult to pull the needle through a seed bead, use your needle-nose pliers to give you a better grip.

variation thistle-bead iridescent danglers

Many variations are possible on this theme. In this variation an eyepin was hung through the beaded bead, and a long iridescent dangle attached beneath the thistle. You could also embellish the thistle with random dots, or loops could replace the fringe.

string of stones

This beautiful necklace is quick and easy to make and can be adapted for many different looks. Although the project uses pearls and gemstones, it can be just as stunning in glass beads or you can make it entirely from silver beads. The impact lies in the quantity of small beads and the cascade of the beads at the neckline.

When choosing bead colours for a necklace, it often helps to study a significant bead that you wish to include. In this example, the stunning mookite faceted nugget that sits at the focal point of the necklace suggested the colouring for the other beads.

before you begin

materials

5.4 kg (12 lb) test weight clear or blue
   fishing line

10 g (⅜ oz) 11° seed beads in iridescent
   bronze or a combination of closely
   related seed beads

5 g (³⁄₁₆ oz) 8° seed beads in 'old time' pink,
   for the accent colour

83 small (maximum size 5 mm/³⁄₁₆ in) beads:
   used here are sunstone beads, gold and
   pink off-round pearls, faceted rhodonite
   rondelles, faceted vintage glass beads
   and bronze Miyuki cubes

30 medium beads (6–10 mm/ ¼–⅜ in):
   faceted pink, bronze and ruby pearls,
   apricot pearl squares, ocean jasper
   stars, ocean jasper rondelles, faceted
   glass beads, stick pearls and 2 or 3
   larger stones (maximum size 30 mm/
   1¼ in): used here are two mookite
   faceted nuggets and one ocean jasper
   flat nugget briolette

tools

   Needle-nose pliers
   Scissors
   Instant-bond glue
   Small clothes pegs or paper clips

making the necklace

1 Cut two lengths of fishing line, 3 m (2¼ yd)
   long. Holding two ends together, string the
briolette into the middle. Working two ends
together on each side, string enough seed beads
on either side of the stone to allow space for the
top of the briolette (about 11 beads). Pull all four
ends through one seed bead, one small bead,
one medium bead and another small bead. You
now have four strands ready for stringing.

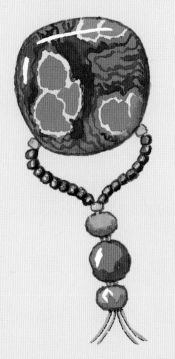

2 String beads along each strand separately
   for 51 cm (20 in), using 11° seed beads with
a mixture of 8° seed beads and smaller beads.
Each strand should also have about six or
seven medium-sized beads. Make sure that all
strands are equal in length and that the bead
size and colours are evenly distributed. Clamp
each strand with a peg when you have finished.

3 Thread all four strands down through a
   large stone. Alternatively, you could use
two or three medium-sized beads to create a
bead grouping (see page 32).

4 Now string each strand separately again,
   interspersing small beads with medium
ones for about 8 cm (3⅛ in). Towards the end of
the strands, make sure you choose beads with
large enough holes to put the fishing line
through twice. End each strand at a slightly
different length, with a large bead or a
grouping, to give the ends weight.
String one more seed bead or an
odd-number grouping (such as
three or five) and then go back
up through your last bead.

5 Pull the fishing line so there is no
   slackness, and then make the first
overhand knot. Go into the next bead and then
make another overhand knot. Continue in this
manner until you have made four or five knots.
Go through one more bead and
then snip the line. Put a tiny
drop of glue on the first
knot. Complete the ends of
the other strands in the
same way.

autumn fire

There are some amazingly complex and beautiful beads made by glass artists. The focal bead on this necklace, by Nancy Tobey, combines many different layers of glass into an organic leaf shape. Designing a necklace around a bead like this is a pleasure. Begin by holding the bead next to other beads to see which are most flattering. Look deep into the bead for hints of less obvious colour choices. Mainly pearls and gems were selected to complement this focal bead but the subtle flashes of amber in its depths influenced the choice of amber seed beads used. The tassel ending contains a variety of weaves. See pages 111–113 for instructions on weaving patterns.

before you begin

materials

For the main strand:

32 x 8 mm (⁵⁄₁₆ in) yellow jade faceted beads
(Bead A)

16 x 5 mm (³⁄₁₆ in) gold potato pearls (Bead B)

8 x 11 mm (⁷⁄₁₆ in) green turquoise peas
(Bead C)

15 x 7 mm (¼ in) ruby-red jade faceted
rondelles (Bead D)

7 x 8 mm (⁵⁄₁₆ in) cranberry faceted pearls
(Bead E)

5 g (³⁄₁₆ oz) 11° gold-lined amber seed beads
(Bead F)

1 x 48 mm (1¾ in) artist's glass bead (or focal
bead with a hole of at least 2 mm/¹⁄₁₆ in)

2 gold-coloured crimp beads

80 cm (32 in) beading wire, .014 diameter

For the tassel strands:

14 x 2 mm (¹⁄₁₆ in) red pearls

1 x 10 mm (⅜ in) jasper star

3 x 6 mm (¼ in) sunstone coin beads

11 x 5 mm (³⁄₁₆ in) gold potato pearls

85 x 11° matt olive-green beads

12 x 11° clear olive-green beads

1 x 7 mm (¼ in) ruby-red jade faceted
rondelle

12 x 11° silver-lined green beads

105 x 11° pale-yellow beads

63 x 11° gold-lined amber beads

90 x 10° vintage bronze tri-cuts

45 x 14° matt brown beads

Neutral-beige nylon beading thread, size D

tools

Pencil

Scissors

Needle-nose pliers

Crimping pliers (optional)

Size 12 sharps needle

Thread conditioner

making the necklace

1 Begin by making your bead tassel. Each strand of the tassel in this project is made up of a different woven chain. Look at pages 111–113 for weaving patterns. To make the tassel strands form a loop (so that you can connect them to the necklace) begin by threading a needle with a long conditioned thread. Working a single thread, leave a 12 cm (5 in) tail and bring the needle up through a rondelle bead and around a pencil. Make a knot to form a loop around the pencil, then bring the needle around the pencil once more and then down through the rondelle.

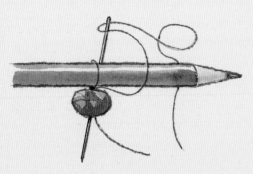

2 Begin weaving a beaded strand to the length you want for your tassel (6–8 cm (2¼–3⅛ in) in the example). Finish with a heavier bead, make an overhand knot, and then work your thread back up your strand to reinforce your weaving. Work the other thread end into the weaving as well and trim the ends.

3 Repeat this procedure for each strand, following the weaving patterns of your choice, so that all the strands form a loop around the pencil. Stagger the ends to slightly different lengths. You can make a tassel with any number of strands, as long as they fit through your rondelle bead. An odd count of five, seven or nine strands works well. When the tassel is complete and all ends are woven in (see page 20), slip the loop off the pencil.

4 Working with an 80 cm (32 in) length of beading wire, pass one end down a rondelle, through the focal bead and through the loop made by the pencil. Move this to the middle of your beading wire and then go back up through the focal bead and rondelle, pulling the tassel loop so it settles against your focal bead.

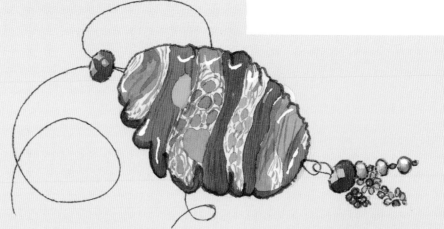

5 String each side. Follow the sequence of beads illustrated below so that it is repeated four times each side, but on one side omit beads D, E, D so that the pattern is continual all the way round.

6 String a crimp bead onto each side, and then bring each strand through opposite sides of beads D, E, D and through the crimp beads. Crush the crimp beads, then work the wire ends into beads and trim.

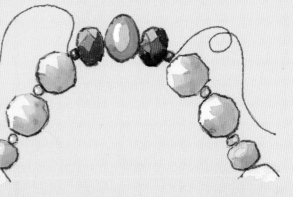

tip

✳ Be sure to stagger the ends of your tassel slightly to maximize the effect of the endings.

tassel weaving

Many simple weaves can be used to create the strands of a tassel. Illustrated here are a selection of simple daisy chains that can be varied by changing the colours and sizes of the beads, or can be combined with different weaves within the same strand. The Simple Chain pattern on page 112 has been used in the Flower Charm Necklace on page 117, and the Pearl Chain pattern using pearls and seed beads on page 112 makes up one of the strands in the Autumn Fire tassel on pages 108–109. The five tassel endings illustrated are just some of the many possibilities.

ten-bead link daisy chain

Here the daisy pattern has been separated by links of ten beads and the central bead in the daisy is slightly larger.

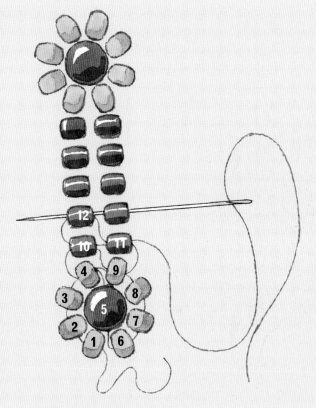

Follow the numbered thread path:
1, 2, 3, 4, 5, 6, 7, 8, 9, 10, 4, 9, 11, 10, 12, 11

two-bead link daisy chain

This daisy chain is separated by a two-bead link (beads 10 and 11) which may be made in another colour so that the daisies are more obvious.

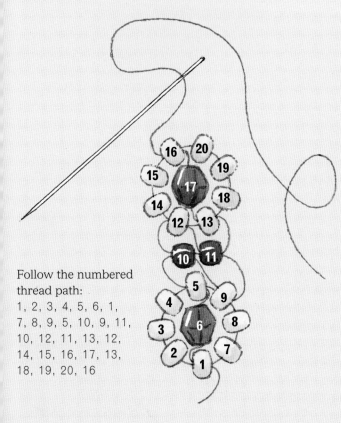

Follow the numbered thread path:
1, 2, 3, 4, 5, 6, 1, 7, 8, 9, 5, 10, 9, 11, 10, 12, 11, 13, 12, 14, 15, 16, 17, 13, 18, 19, 20, 16

simple chain

This straightforward pattern can create a thicker chain than the daisy pattern, but if the outer beads are smaller it can take on a delicate vine-like look.

Follow the numbered thread path:
1, 2, 3, 4, 5, 6, 7, 1, 2, 3, 4, 8, 9, 10, 11, 12, 3, 4, 8, 9, 13, 14, 15, 16, 17, 4, 3, 2, 1

pearl chain

Pearls and seed beads can be alternated to create a charming chain.

single-stem daisy chain

This is another daisy chain but in this case there are single beads between the daisies rather than links.

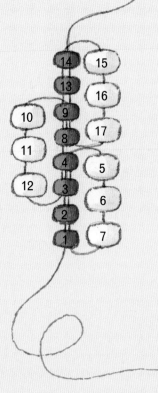

large bead ending
A heavy bead makes a good ending. Its weight straightens the tassel and it gives a satisfying jangle as it moves against the other tassels.

star bead ending
This star bead could finish with just one seed bead or with a small loop.

woven leaf ending
A leaf shape can be woven from seed beads to create a special ending.

Follow the numbered thread path:
1, 2, 3, 4, 5, 6, 7, 8, 9, 10, 1, 11, 3, 12, 5, 13, 14, 15, 7, 16, 9, 17, 18, 11, 19, 12, 20, 13, 14, 21, 22, 21, 14, 15, 23, 16, 24, 17, 25, 1,

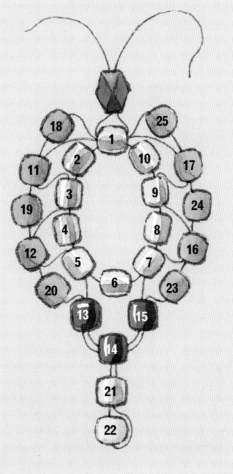

loop ending
A loop at the end of an interesting bead such as a pearl is a good way to add weight and length to the tassel.

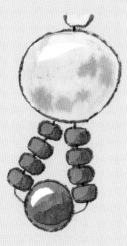

simple loop ending
This is the simplest ending for a tassel. Make sure that the first bead has some weight.

silver seeds

variations leaf charm and flower charm necklace

This bracelet reminds me of the time of year when I start working in the garden. It is still cold and the branches are bare, but there is great beauty in the shapes and colours of the plants before they burst into life.

The steely colours of this bracelet are contemporary and it would appeal to someone who likes to wear silver jewellery. Alternatively, you could omit the silver beads and use a bronze iris hex bead with a red and bronze colour scheme. When the bracelet is worn, it looks like a frill of leaves around your wrist.

before you begin

materials

5 g (³⁄₁₆ oz) 11° beads, frosted rainbow
   cranberry (Bead A)

1 x 41 cm (16 in) strand of 2–2.5 mm (¹⁄₁₆ in)
   faceted silver beads (Bead B)
   You can substitute a twisted-hex bead
   or another cylinder-shaped bead for B

5 g (³⁄₁₆ oz) 11° beads, translucent oily blue-
   iris (Bead C)

5 g (³⁄₁₆ oz) 11° beads, silver-lined light-blue
   matt (Bead D)

5 g (³⁄₁₆ oz) 11° beads, aqua-blue tri-cuts
   (Bead E)

Alternatively, you can use just one colour
   of bead for D and E

5 g (³⁄₁₆ oz) 14° beads, opaque blue-grey matt
   (Bead F)

Grey nylon beading thread, size D

1 beaded button (follow the directions on
   pages 90–91) using beads E and F

tools

Size 13 sharps needle

Needle-nose pliers

Beeswax and thread conditioner

Liquid seam sealant

making the bracelet

1 Working with a single, conditioned thread, leave a 6 cm (2⅜ in) tail and thread a stopper bead on your work (see page 9). Begin with one silver cylinder bead (bead 1) followed by 12 A beads. Go back through beads 3 and 4 and add one more bead A. Repeat this sequence 18 more times (there are 19 leaves on the bracelet).

2 Make a square knot with the single thread and trim it, leaving a 10 cm (4 in) tail to weave in later. Change to doubled, waxed thread (see page 20). String one silver bead, one bead A and one silver bead, and then make a loop large enough to fit around your beaded button (about 38 beads) with bead A. Work one row of peyote stitch (see page 22) around this loop using an occasional blue bead.

3 Working back through your bracelet, weave each sequence as illustrated. Beads 15, 16 and 17 are C, 18 is A, and 19, 20 and 21 are C. Continue until the last leaf.

4 When you have added bead 21 on your last leaf, loop your thread around the threads between beads 4 and 14 of your first leaf and begin the next row.

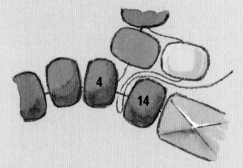

5 Follow the illustration below to the other end of the bracelet using D beads. Go around the button loop with your thread so that you are facing in the right direction to make your final row.

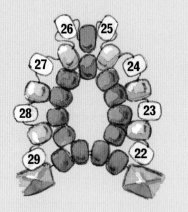

6 To finish the leaves, follow the illustration below. Beads 30–33 are E, 34 is B, 35 is F, 36–39 are E. When you come to the last leaf continue out through bead 1 and remove the stopper bead. Add one bead A, before you make a loop to hang your button on. The bracelet in the example measures 19.5 cm (7½ in) long. If you would like it longer, you can add extra beads before you begin the loop. Make a loop of 17 beads through the button shank. Bring your thread back around the loop twice more to strengthen it. Knot your thread, apply a drop of seam sealant to your needle tip and weave in the thread ends (see page 20).

tips

❊ Threads can twist around each other and get caught in knots. To minimize this problem, work with a well-waxed double thread or a conditioned single thread. Occasionally hold your work up with the needle dangling so that the thread can untwist.

❊ Pull thread through beads slowly so that you have time to catch knots before they form.

❊ If a knot appears, use tweezers and patience to unpick it gently.

variations leaf charm and flower charm necklace

leaf charm

Following the steps for the main project, small leaf and flower charms can be made. To make a leaf charm, begin by creating a loop of approximately seven beads, then repeat the leaf sequence three times and finish.

flower charm necklace

This necklace is made by weaving beads using the Simple Chain pattern on page 112, interspersed with rice pearls, and adding a flower pendant. The pendant has a blue pearl hanging in the middle. To make a flower, work five leaves in a circle with a loop coming from the top of one of them. The middle can be left open, a bead can dangle inside or a button can be sewn into the centre.

tickled pink tassel
variation embellished tassel

Tassels can be made with one large bead at the top as in the Autumn Fire necklace on pages 108–110, or they can be made with an integrated beaded cap. This tassel has a beaded cap with embellishment. The stripes in the tassel fringe look wonderful in movement but also look attractive hanging from a doorknob when not being worn.

The instructions for this project may appear long but they are straightforward to follow. The main difficulty is that the thread can become tangled in the fringes. Wrap the fringes with a strip of cloth if they get in the way.

before you begin

materials

15 g (½ oz) 14° opaque matt brown with
    purple, blue, gold and green iridescent
    beads (Bead A)

10 g (⅜ oz) 14° silver-lined translucent fuchsia
    beads (Bead B)

5 g (³⁄₁₆ oz) 11° silver-lined fuchsia beads
    (Bead C)

5 g (³⁄₁₆ oz) 11° beads similar in colour to
    Bead A (Bead D)

110 x 3 mm (⅛ in) bronze pearls

14 x 12 mm (½ in) faceted oval rhodonite
    stones

Nylon beading thread in a colour to match
    Bead A, size 0 or 00

Nylon beading thread in a colour to match
    Bead A, size D

1 m (39 in) fine beading wire, size .014

2 crimp beads

tools

Needle-nose pliers

Crimping pliers (optional)

Beeswax and thread conditioner

Size 12 sharps needle and beading needle

Scissors

making the necklace

1 First make the tassel. You need to create a honeycomb of beads from which to hang the fringes. This core honeycomb will have many passes of thread and needle so begin with bead D and very fine beading thread on the size 12 sharps needle. Work with a single strand of conditioned thread. Pick up two 11° beads and go back through the first, leaving a 10 cm (4 in) tail. Adjust them so they lie side by side.

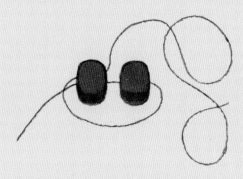
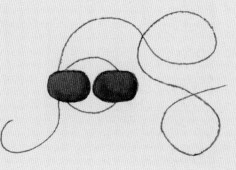

2 Add another bead and come back up through the first bead. Continue doing this until you have six beads radiating from the first bead.

3 Follow the illustration of the thread path for securing the beads. Do not pull the thread too tightly during your first round; the beads need to lie flat.

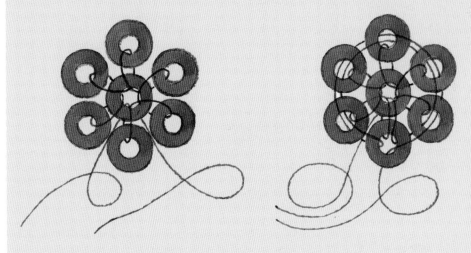

4 Add a third round of beads in the same manner but increase by adding two beads for each bead on round 2. Secure the beads in a flat circle by weaving in and out of them as you did with the second round.

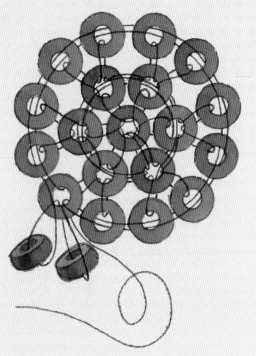

5 To make the fourth and final round, repeat step 4, but this time increase only every other bead. Secure beads in a flat circle as you did before.

6 You are now ready to begin making the fringes. Switch to a beading needle and the size D nylon thread. Work with a single, waxed thread. Bring your needle down through the first bead in the honeycomb. For the central strand with the rhodonite stone, string beads in a repeat of seven A beads, two B beads until they reach about 8 cm (3¼ in). Add three C beads, one pearl, one rhodonite stone, one pearl, one bead B, one bead C, one bead B and then back up through the pearl, stone, pearl, all the seed beads, and out the top of the first bead in the honeycomb. Make a knot to secure the strand.

7 Continue adding a fringe through each of the beads in the honeycomb. Follow the sequence in step 6, but in each round on the honeycomb, reduce the length of the fringe by one repeat so that the ends of the tassel are staggered. All these fringes end with three C beads, one pearl, one bead B, and then back through the pearl and seed beads. There will be 37 fringes in total.

8 You now begin building the beaded bead top to the tassel with brick stitch (see page 22). You will cover it completely with embellishments so this step will be invisible in the final tassel. Using doubled waxed nylon thread and a size 12 sharps, bring your needle out through the top of one of the beads in round 4. Using bead D, begin by stringing two beads, then pass your needle through the second exposed loop and back up your second bead.

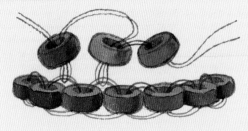

9 Continue adding one bead at a time in this manner, each time going through the next exposed loop until you have added the last bead. Bring your needle down through the first bead and secure it to the loop beneath it, come back up that bead and string two more beads to begin the next row.

10 To give your tassel top shape make the following decreases:

Row 4: one decrease every 6 beads, 15 beads total

Row 7: one decrease every 5 beads, 12 beads total

Row 9: one decrease every 3 beads, 9 beads total

Row 10, final row: decrease to 4 or 5 beads.

To make a decrease follow the illustration below.

11 To embellish the tassel top begin at the bottom. Bring the needle up through one of the D beads, add three C beads and then come back up through the next bead. Carry on around the whole row.

12 Switch to A beads and complete three more rows the same way. Skip a row and then add two B beads, one C bead, two B beads to each bead in the next row. Skip the next row and then add three A beads to each bead in the final three rows. Look over the bead to see if there are any gaps in the beading; embellish these if there are.

13 Bring the needle back out the top of the tassel bead, string five A beads, one pearl, five A beads, one pearl, five A beads and then go back down through the centre, all the way to the fringed side of the honeycomb. Go through a different bead in the honeycomb that you came out of and go back up to reinforce the loop. Embellish around the base of the loop with B beads.

14 String a necklace to hang the tassel from. Clamp one end of the beading wire and thread on five C beads, one pearl, five C beads, one pearl, five C beads, one pearl, five C beads, one pearl, one rhodonite stone, one pearl. Repeat 11 more times, threading the tassel onto the necklace between the sixth and seventh rhodonite stones.

15 To finish the necklace, thread on five C beads and one pearl three times. Thread on five more C beads, then string a crimp bead onto each side. Bring each strand through the opposite sides of the final rhodonite stone and through the crimp beads. Crush the crimp beads, then work the wire ends into the beads and trim.

tips

❋ Never use tape to hold your bead fringe out of the way. Once the sticky coating is on the beads it is impossible to remove. Use a strip of cloth tied or taped instead.

❋ To make a fuller beaded cap, weave a larger honeycomb, increasing every third bead for round 5.

❋ You can make the ends of the tassel shorter but they should not extend any longer unless you make the bead cap bigger as well.

variation embellished tassel

Many embellishing variations are possible; both to the fringes and the bead cap. Consider adding bugle beads, drops or daggers to the fringe. The beads can have netting or other variations of fringe in the final layer. Beads on the interior of the fringe can be a different colour from the final layer. Experiment with variations in the bead cap embellishment. In this example, a beaded star hangs from the longest fringe in the tassel.

jewel jangles
variation autumn charm bracelet

This charm cuff has four strands and an attractive woven closure. It moves nicely and creates lots of space to show off beads and buttons. Because it is worn close fitting, it is a good place to include decorative buttons, as they will stay right-side showing. This example includes flameworked dot glass beads, vintage Bakelite buttons and 1930s' pressed glass. The ruby colour of the seed beads allows a wide variety of rich colours to blend beautifully with each other.

before you begin

materials

Nylon beading thread in a colour to match your colour scheme, size D

80 x 2.2 mm (1/16 in) bronze twisted-hex beads

5 g (3/16 oz) 12° ruby iris tri-cuts (if you use another bead, make sure the fishing line can fit through the hole twice and that the bead's length is roughly half the length of the twisted-hex)

1 beaded button (see pages 88–91), or button of your choice, not more than 18 mm (3/4 in) in diameter

Enough beads and headpins to make about eight charms. Consider using beads, beaded stars, leaves, flowers and beaded beads

About 30 small (under 5 mm/3/16 in) fancy beads

About 15 beads or buttons 5–15 mm (3/16–9/16 in)

2 m (6½ ft) fishing line, 5.4 kg (12 lb) test weight

tools

Beeswax or thread conditioner

Size 12 sharps needle

Needle-nose pliers

Scissors

Instant-bond glue

Small clothes pegs or paper clips

making the bracelet

1 Once you have selected a pile of beads in colours you like, make up about eight charms following directions for putting beads on headpins and eyepins (pages 66–67), or making beaded stars (pages 94–95), beads (pages 82–87), or flowers and leaves (pages 96–98 and 114–116).

2 Before you begin stringing the beads, make up the woven ends using square stitch (see page 22). Working with waxed doubled thread, thread on a stopper bead (see page 9), and follow the illustration below, using twisted-hex beads and tri-cuts to create the first two rows.

3 These rows need reinforcing because they will hold all the beading work. Follow the thread path below to go back through all the beads, finally exiting from bead 10.

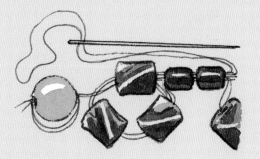

tips

✳ You can decide on the placement of charms on headpins when you have finished making up the bracelet.

✳ Close the ends of headpins and eyepins tightly so they do not slip off the fishing line.

✳ You can bead all the strands before deciding to tie them off. Use clamps or pegs to keep the beads in place when you are not working on them.

4 The beads in row 2 may be filled with thread and difficult to get your needle through for the next row. If this is the case, attach the thread between the beads rather than going through them.

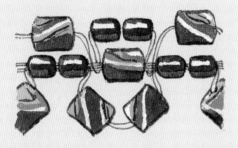

5 If the thread can fit through the bead holes in row 2 follow the thread path shown below to row 13.

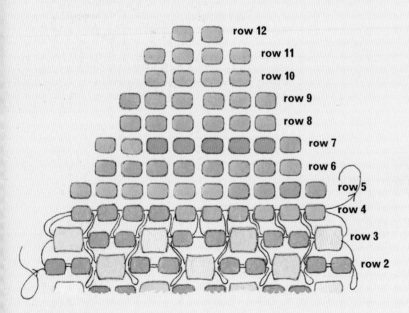

6 Reinforce rows 12 and 13 by taking your thread through a second time. After the final bead in row 13, make a beaded loop big enough for your button. Reinforce the loop by taking the thread through again, then make a knot and weave in the ends (see page 20). Create a second woven end, attaching the button instead of a loop.

7 To make the four beaded strands, begin by looping the fishing line around the threads between the pairs of twisted-hexes at the end of the triangles. Bring both ends of the fishing line through a seed bead and make a knot. Do this two more times.

8 Put a drop of instant-bond glue on one of the knots and move the beads as close to the bead weaving as you can. Continue stringing along both threads for a few more beads and then trim one thread off. Continue stringing, using a variety of beads and about two charms per strand. When you reach a length that, when attached to the second end, will give you a measurement of 19 cm (7½ in) (or suitable for your wrist, see page 32) prepare to end beading.

9 The illustration below shows which threads end at which terminus. To finish the strand, repeat the sequence of wrapping the thread around the middle of the pairs of hexes, bringing it back through a bead and making a knot. Do this two more times, and apply a drop of glue to one of the knots.

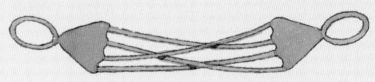

10 Repeat this for the other three strands, staggering large beads, buttons and charms. Before you cut the ends, put the cuff on to check the bead placement.

variation autumn charm bracelet

The rich bronze of the antique cut-glass button used here suggested the colour scheme for this variation. Several vintage buttons have been mixed with beaded stars and other charms to make a very unique bracelet.

index

acknowledgements

Author's acknowledgements:
I would like to thank Katie Saunders for her help with the beadwork. Katie, you could make any work fun!

The beads came from many sources but I would particularly like to thank Nancy Tobey, Empyrean beads, Beads Forever, Happy Mango Beads, Splendor in the Glass, and the Beadin Path for their supplies and help.

Publisher's acknowledgements:
Executive editor Sarah Tomley
Editor Alice Bowden
Executive art editor Rozelle Bentheim
Designer Maggie Town
Illustrator Kate Simunek
Photographer Donna Eaves
Senior production controller Manjit Sihra